Violins & Shovels

The WPA Arts Projects

MILTON MELTZER

Violins & Shovels

The WPA Arts Projects

DELACORTE PRESS / NEW YORK

Picture Researcher: Olivia Buehl

Designed by Giorgetta Bell McRee

Library of Congress Cataloging in Publication Data

Meltzer, Milton, 1915–
Violins and shovels.

Bibliography: p.
Includes index.
SUMMARY: Examines arts projects run during the 1930's
which were funded by the Works Progress Administration.
1. Federal aid to the arts—United States. 2. Arts,
Modern—20th century—United States. 3. United States.
Works Progress Administration. [1. United States. Works
Progress Administration. 2. Federal aid to the arts]
I. Title.
NX735.M44   700'.973   75-32916

ISBN 0-440-09316-3

For Victor Keller

Contents

1. ROCK BOTTOM *1*

2. ON RELIEF *9*

3. VIOLINS AND SHOVELS *16*

4. A THEATER THAT TAKES CHANCES *23*

5. THE LIVING NEWSPAPER VERSUS
   THE DEADLY CENSOR *31*

6. SHAW AND O'NEILL: 55 CENTS *45*

7. THE PAINTER AND THE TIME CLOCK *53*

8. AN ALMOST INFINITE VARIETY *62*

9. ART FOR THE PEOPLE *76*

10. MUSIC IN THE AIR *91*

11. LITERARY SHARECROPPERS *100*

12. UNCOVERING AMERICA *108*

13. FOLK LIFE IN BLACK AND WHITE *120*

14. PINK SLIPS *132*

15. FINALE OR OVERTURE? *142*

BIBLIOGRAPHY *150*

INDEX *154*

1 ROCK BOTTOM

The thirties? That was the time when I was growing up. As the decade of the Great Depression opened, I had entered my second year in high school. Worcester, Massachusetts, an industrial town, was about to suffer hard times. But at the age of fifteen it took me a while to feel the impact the Depression would have on the lives of friends and neighbors.

The stock market crash in the fall of 1929 was no signal of disaster to the family of a window cleaner. My father washed the windows of factories, stores, offices, and homes. Their owners held some of the stocks that tumbled so disastrously—$26 billion—in the first month of the Depression. But we owned no stocks and didn't even know what they were. All we owned were our clothes and the furniture of the tenement we lived in.

Our family did not "go broke" in the Depression. We started broke. My father and mother were immigrants from Eastern Europe. They had little education and no job training. My father was a one-man business. He did all the work. My older brother made out the bills for him until I took over the monthly chore. My mother ran the household—cooking, baking, cleaning, washing, ironing, sewing, shopping, and worrying.

Soon enough we found out that you didn't have to own stocks to feel the impact of the crash. The shock wave spread rapidly from Wall Street to the poorest unskilled worker. More than 100,000 businesses suddenly failed. By the end of 1931, when I became a junior at Classical High School, 7 million people had been thrown out of work. By the time I graduated, the number was over 15 million.

When the crash came, it wasn't the rich who became poor. The "big rich," owners of the great American fortunes, were able to hang onto their money. Below them were the prosperous Americans. They lived better than 95 percent of the people. In those days it took only $6,000 a year to be prosperous. It sounds small today, but in 1929 we didn't know anyone who earned that kind of money. Almost four out of five families earned less than $3,000 a year. And about a third of this group had incomes below $1,000 a year. Miners and lumbermen, doing hard, dirty, dangerous work, earned only about $10 a week.

My family was sandwiched somewhere in those lower layers. We could save nothing at all. The only way we could add to the bare necessities of life was by buying on credit—"a dollar down, and a dollar forever."

If the twenties were so prosperous, where had the money gone? The cream was skimmed off at the top. The richest Americans—the 5 percent at the top—controlled about one-third of all personal income. They invested their money at high interest rates and paid almost no income tax. I remember reading in a gossip column that it was the habit of some celebrity to tip his waiter at the Plaza Hotel in New York a twenty-dollar bill. My father would have had to clean 133 windows (at 15 cents apiece) to earn that much money.

As factories cut down production and stores were boarded up, there were fewer and fewer windows to clean. My father, whose day began at two in the morning and often did not end until late afternoon, was home more and more for lack of work. Extra jobs, even the oddest ones, were hard to find. The telephone company fired twenty married women because their husbands had jobs. The best my older brother, my mother, and I could do was to get part-time work that lasted briefly and paid poorly. Still, we managed to eat. Food was cheaper then, and the Depression drove prices even lower. At the corner grocery, eggs were 19 cents a dozen; lettuce, a nickel a head; whole-wheat bread, a nickel a loaf; bananas, 8 cents a dozen; mackerel, two pounds for a quarter; beef, 11 cents a pound; and tomato soup, three cans for 19 cents.

By the winter of 1931, there were men in our neighborhood who had been out of work for months. When Lake Quinsigamond froze, my friend's father was lucky enough to get temporary work harvesting the ice in a crew of jobless men hired by the city employment bureau.

And relief, what was that? There were no plans for public welfare. There was no such thing as unemployment insurance. President Herbert Hoover, sitting in the White House, expected private philanthropy to take care of the unemployed. But the spread of suffering at last obliged him to set up a committee. All it did was urge people to tighten their belts. It didn't even gather facts about how many were jobless and in need of help.

By my last year in high school, 1932, one-fourth of the nation—men, women, and children—belonged to families with no regular income. And almost nothing was being done to provide them with relief. Wealthy businessmen were against any national measure that would raise their federal income tax.

The cities, counties, and states were not prepared to meet the crisis. Even when they meant well, few had enough funds to offer relief. Where they did, many proud people refused to take it. They believed it was their own fault if they lost a job. They were ashamed to accept help.

Only federal money could fill the hungry bellies. And as late as 1932, President Hoover was saying, "What this country needs is a great poem. Something to lift people out of fear and selfishness. . . . Sometimes a great poem can do more than legislation."

It could thrill the soul, perhaps, but it couldn't feed the hungry. In the Worcester *Telegram* I read about a man who had gone into a downtown restaurant, ordered oysters, salad, a steak, pie, ice cream, and coffee. After finishing his meal, he called the manager and said, "Now you can put me in jail. This was my first meal in three days. I haven't got a dime."

A few days later, our newspaper reported that a twenty-two-year-old man had shot his fiancée, killing her when she returned his engagement ring. Her parents had forced her to break off with him because he had failed to find work for more than a year, and had no prospects. On another page, a headline announced, COMEDY PICTURES WILL HOLD SWAY. PRODUCERS PLAN TO ROUT GLOOM WITH LAUGHS.

Eight inches of snow fell toward the end of that year of 1931. A blessing for the jobless. The city hired those with dependent families to clear the streets. In Washington, Senator William Borah said that until the hungry were fed and relief provided, not another bill would pass the Senate.

But the President stood firm. The proposal for relief hit at the country's roots, he said.

A week later, the Communist party demonstrated for unemployment insurance and public relief in New York, Boston, Washington, Hartford, and Worcester. Coming home from school I passed the Common behind City Hall and saw about seventy-five men and women, ringed by half as many police. The demonstrators carried hand-lettered signs calling for free gas, coal, electricity, food, and clothing for needy families. I watched a man mount a soapbox and yell up toward the windows of Mayor O'Hara, "Put us to work! There are twelve thousand unemployed people in Worcester, and you offer us three jobs shoveling snow! We don't ask charity. We want work! If the capitalists won't give us jobs, give us the means to live!"

The police listened quietly. The man got down from his soapbox and carried it away. I drifted on home. A month later, the mayor asked city employees to give a percentage of their pay to the unemployed. If they refused, he said, he would cut their pay. But that month there was no pay— not for the mayor and not for any other city workers. The town's treasury had temporarily gone dry.

Just before Christmas recess about 1,500 hungry marchers reached Washington and found the doors of the White House and the Capitol barred to them. A classmate told me that his father, who had worked on the railroad all his life, was being asked to take a 10 percent pay cut. Would he? "Sure," said Al, "it's that or a bunch of them being fired."

Perhaps as a generous Christmas gesture, City Hall announced that twenty-six more men would be given apple-selling posts. There were so many men out on the streets selling apples for a nickel apiece that Worcester had to regulate the trade. A week later, on page 1, the *Telegram* announced that nine Massachusetts banks had closed, including the local Bancroft Trust Company.

Then it was New Year's Day, 1932.

"Remember the year 1931 as a year of disaster," said the *Telegram* in its lead editorial. "The storm of depression which broke late in '29, which swept with cumulative force through 1930 and finally reached a crescendo of evil in 1931—that storm people will try to forget with the facility which human psychology gives for casting bad memories out of the mind. . . ."

Forget? On the next page was a story headlined, CHILDREN STARVE IN COAL DISTRICTS OF WEST VIRGINIA AND KENTUCKY.

It was our senior year in high school. Some of the kids joked about whether the school would last long enough to let us graduate. After all, Chicago, an infinitely bigger city, had just shut down its schools because of lack of funds. Their teachers had not been paid for months.

A new mayor took office in Worcester. The Honorable John C. Mahoney said in his inaugural address that the biggest task he faced was relief. The city was now spending more for that than on its fire and police departments.

The next day a sixty-five-year-old man, a retired broker now penniless, shot himself. The mayor's own staff took a 10 percent cut. Needy men were put to work cleaning out the Quinapoxet reservoir basin.

By the middle of January, the governor of Massachusetts was warning the cities that funds were so low they must cut down on relief. Our mayor slashed relief costs by 10 percent. He said he would no longer pay rent for jobless families unless landlords issued eviction notices and people were about to be put out on the street.

In February, a young, university-trained actress who had

gone to Broadway full of hope and ambition, came back to Worcester. She had failed to find even a walk-on role in a starving theater. She sat silently at home for a few weeks, then took a trolley car out to Lake Quinsigamond, chopped a hole in the ice, and drowned herself.

The last story of that winter I care to remember is that of Albert Fortin and Pasquale Furtaldo. Albert, twenty-three, had not eaten for several days. He saw Pasquale, fifteen, leave a grocery store carrying a loaf of bread and a bottle of milk. He followed the boy home and as Pasquale was about to enter his house, seized an ax and struck him on the head. Frightened by his own violence, he dragged the boy to the rear of the house, and then fled, without the bread and milk. A few hours later he surrendered to the police.

In March, Detroit, Michigan, which seemed so remote from New England in those days, suddenly was as close as the day's headline. Unemployed auto workers marched on Henry Ford's factory, and four men were murdered in a volley of police bullets. Throughout the Midwest, farmers were banding together. They threatened to shoot anyone who would foreclose their mortgages. In Iowa, angry farmers had dragged a foreclosing judge off the bench and beat him unconscious. Right here at home, Arthur Thornby, the owner of a downtown restaurant, had disappeared. He left a note for his wife, saying his debts had piled so high he couldn't go on.

Our mayor ordered streetlights to be dimmed to save money on power. As the lights went down, a shock ran through our neighborhood. The motorman on a trolley line we all used was held up by two boys. They had boarded the trolley and sat quietly in the rear until the end of the run. After all the other passengers got off, they pulled out a gun and took $8 in fares from the motorman.

Everybody knew Paul and Leo. No one had ever expected they would do something like that. What would happen to them now?

At school, the senior year rolled on, and we ignored the world outside. A class dance, the basketball and hockey games, electioneering for office. No athlete, but a "word man," I made the debating team and the yearbook board, and wound up elected class prophet. Old and wise as I felt at seventeen, I never could have prophesied what was about to happen.

2 ON RELIEF

The biggest thing in my life then was the chance to go to college. A New York school had accepted me, and by combining a scholarship, job, loan, and a few dollars a week from my father's meager earnings, it looked like I might at least make a start. I sweated through that summer in New York, earning money as an unskilled worker in an uncle's garment shop. Riding the bus to work each morning, I saw strung along the Hudson River shore hundreds of shacks made of tin cans, packing crates, cardboard, and old tar paper. They were no bigger than chicken coops, these rent-free homes, and their tenants had named them Hoovervilles in honor of the President.

As that hot and lonely summer wore on, the papers were showing Hoovervilles of another kind sprawled on the outskirts of Washington, D.C. Nearly 20,000 veterans, dubbed the Bonus Army, had flooded into the capital to demand payment of a veterans bonus authorized by Congress in 1924 but not due until 1945. Over a quarter of a million ex-soldiers—jobless and hungry—needed that money now. But Hoover opposed paying them. They lived in all kinds of cockeyed lean-tos scraped together from the city dump. Congress quit for the summer without paying them their bonus, but the vets hung on. Then Hoover ordered infantry, cavalry, tanks, and machine guns to get rid of them. The unarmed vets with their wives and children were bayoneted and gassed, their shelters burned, their food destroyed, and two of them were shot dead. They fled Washington, stumbling along the roads back to where they had come from. A reporter for the St. Louis *Post-Dispatch* wrote that Hoover's purpose was "to show the country that the danger of 'insurrection' was real and that the Administration had prepared to meet it."

Early that summer the Republicans renominated Hoover for President, and the Democrats chose Franklin D. Roosevelt as their candidate. It wasn't at all clear from the campaign speeches what Roosevelt would do. But while Hoover's tone was mournful, FDR's radiated confidence in his ability to make things better. *He* isn't going to let people starve, I thought.

Soon after classes started in the fall, Roosevelt was elected. In those days presidents didn't take office until the following March. While FDR and the country waited for inauguration day, "that Austrian corporal," Adolf Hitler, took over in Germany. I remember a cold January night at a professor's house when we students hung over his shortwave radio, unable to believe the hysteria vomiting from Hitler's throat and the roar of his audience's response.

On the eve of Roosevelt's taking office, we dropped into the bottommost pit of the Depression. Losing all confidence in banks, people made a panicky rush to withdraw their money. The banking system of the whole country collapsed overnight. That was where we stood the day FDR took up his duties. For three years we had suffered a tragedy even more bitter than war. In war the enemy was visible, knowable. The anguish and frustration of the Depression came from forces we could not identify, could not fight. Millions had lost material possessions and had forgotten the skills necessary to work. Their health suffered, and worst of all, their pride and self-respect.

Almost frantic with despair, we waited to hear the President's inaugural address. In ringing words he said, "The only thing we have to fear is fear itself." He promised "action and action now" and a "New Deal" for all Americans. And at once he moved so powerfully that it was possible to hope again. In the first hundred days of his administration, more major measures were signed into law than in any comparable period in our history. From the universities, from the schools of law, engineering, and social work, FDR drew hundreds of advisers to Washington to take part in the stupendous task of saving a nation. My campus was but one of many that saw dozens of its best brains disappear into New Deal agencies.

The basic decision was a simple one. In a time of crisis, the federal government would take economic responsibility for its citizens. This was new; this was human. Unlike Hoover, FDR was open-minded. He had no packaged policy to guide a program. But he knew that the human problems of the Great Depression had to be solved. And he was willing to experiment, to try something new if the old ways didn't work.

I did not follow every move the President made. I was on my own for the first time in my seventeen years, and that was troublesome enough. Everyone in my class was a stranger to me, and I did not make friends easily. Then there was New York itself, a monstrous city to a boy from a New England town. The college I was in was experimental—part of its program called for students to spend a year working in industry or on a farm. I went back to

Worcester for my second year, living again at home. Somehow I found a miserable job in a factory, painting women's shoes with a spray gun. On Saturdays I sold shoes to workers and farmers in a cheap store that paid me $2 for the twelve-hour day. And evenings I read voraciously, keeping careful notes to show my instructors.

In the fall of 1934, I returned to school, which was now swept by fevered discussions. Many of my professors were either deeply committed to the New Deal or radical critics of its shortcomings. And so I became more sensitive to what was going on in the larger world. The New Deal was in trouble because it had not brought about economic recovery. So far it had failed to improve the lot of workers, tenant farmers, old people, or small business. Above all, there was still an enormously large number of unemployed. What FDR had done was to pump relief funds into the states and to stimulate the construction industry with a federal public works program. By these means, he hoped to take the federal government out of the relief business altogether. He had also tried direct work relief. One such agency was the Civilian Conservation Corps (CCC), which enrolled some 300,000 young men throughout the country. As part of FDR's ardent conservation program, they did reforestation and other work in the national parks.

By the middle of 1934, the nationwide support FDR had enjoyed when he took office had crumbled. The industrialists, the business and financial leaders had turned against him. They charged he was wrecking constitutional government, coddling labor, and spending the country into bankruptcy. The radicals, on the other hand, accused him of being a tool of Wall Street. But in the November elections to Congress, the Democrats found mass support among workers, farmers, blacks, and other ethnic groups.

By a huge majority, the Democrats took over both houses of Congress.

"This is our hour," said Harry Hopkins, a progressive social worker who had become one of FDR's closest advisers. He favored work relief as opposed to cash relief. Taking leadership of the new left-of-center majority, Roosevelt launched a $5-billion work relief program. In April, 1935, Congress established the Works Progress Administration (WPA), and FDR made Harry Hopkins its director. It was Hopkins who said, "Hunger is not debatable."

The WPA replaced earlier emergency programs. It was like a separate economic system that ran parallel to the regular one. If you couldn't find a job in the private economy, you could try the WPA. It was open to people who did almost anything—ditchdiggers, secretaries, plumbers, lawyers, teachers, salesmen, clerks, nurses.

A dole, Roosevelt said, was "a narcotic, a subtle destroyer of the human spirit. . . . I am not willing that the vitality of our people be further sapped by the giving of cash, of market baskets, of a few hours of weekly work cutting grass, raking leaves or picking up papers in the public parks." The WPA's hope was not only to keep people alive but to put them to work doing what they were trained to do. It wanted to *use* their skills, not keep people busy at meaningless make-work.

As I began my last year in college, private employment was still hard to find. It was 1935, the fifth year of the Depression. Eight million Americans still had no jobs. Nearly 3 million youths between sixteen and twenty-four years of age were on relief. The surface signs of the Depression had almost disappeared, however: no apple sellers on the streets, breadlines gone, the Hoovervilles vanished. But I knew many young men and women who had finished college and had failed to find work. Some had gone back home to live with their families. Some were bumming around the country. And a few, the lucky ones, had landed jobs on the WPA.

I began to feel it was no use going on with my studies. In the papers I read that one-third of the previous year's graduating class had been unable to find any work at all, and another third had gotten jobs for which they had no interest, talent, or training. Going the rounds of the campus was an "Ode to Higher Education":

> I sing in praise of college,
> of MAs and PhDs,
> But in pursuit of knowledge
> We are starving by degrees.

Toward the end of my senior year, I dropped out of college. My father had cancer, and died that fall. I found a place on the West Side of New York City, in the Chelsea neighborhood. The rent was $3 a week. Stepping through the front door of the brownstone was like entering a public urinal. At the top of five flights of stairs was a room almost narrow enough for me to touch the walls with outstretched arms. There was an iron cot, no sheets, a frayed army blanket, a rocklike pillow, a wooden folding chair, a rickety wardrobe that leaned menacingly over me, and a single window through whose smeary glass I could barely see the brick walls of the tenement opposite.

I applied for help at the city's relief bureau. I cannot remember how many days I waited before an investigator came. It felt terribly long because I was so nervous. But at last I qualified, and the relief began coming. The city paid my rent, and every other Friday gave me $5.50. That was what I lived on. Dinner was a cheese sandwich and a cup of coffee. Price—20 cents. When rain or snow began squishing up through the holes in my shoes, I couldn't afford to repair them. My brother showed me how to take the pulpy separators out of egg cartons and stuff them into my shoes for protection. A few months later my luck changed. The Federal Theatre Project gave me a job.

3 VIOLINS AND SHOVELS

I reported for work at a beat-up Greek temple on Eighth Avenue near Forty-fourth Street. The building had once been the home of the Bank of the United States. It had failed late in 1930, to the despair of nearly half a million depositors—many of them immigrants. Because of its name, they had thought it was the government's own bank, and as safe as America herself. Now it was the headquarters of the Federal Theatre of New York. The dismal rooms swarmed with people of incredible variety—actors, directors, stagehands, vaudevillians, puppeteers, dancers, circus performers, scene painters, costumers, makeup artists, technicians, clerks, accountants—and writers.

Which is where I came in. When I applied for home relief, I listed myself as an unemployed writer. It was a bold claim to make on the basis of a few pieces published in the college press and in some magazines of limited circulation. I had to put something down, however, and I wanted very much to become a professional writer. My older brother had had some experience as a publicity writer in New York, had gone on relief, and had then been given a Federal Theatre job in the press department. His function was to help provide information about the project to the media.

One corner of the press department housed a tiny group of writers who wrote stories explaining the project to teachers and students. Many Federal Theatre productions were performed in the schools and pupils often came in organized groups to attend the performances in our theaters. Perhaps because I had some writing samples to show, the head of this division asked for me. (He may have been prodded a bit by my brother.)

My pay was $23.86 a week. It was the salary everyone got who came from the relief rolls and could qualify as a "senior research worker." It was called a "security wage." This meant we were paid *more* than the sum doled out for direct relief, but *less* than the prevailing union wage—to encourage us to return to private jobs as soon as we could find them. The projects adjusted the number of hours people worked to satisfy the unions, which did not like to see their wage structure undercut.

Ninety percent of the workers on the various arts projects came from local relief rolls. A 10 percent exemption from relief qualification was allowed for the supervisory staff, whose pay was higher, but not enough to make them rich. The national director of the Federal Theatre Project, Hallie Flanagan, got $6,000 a year (later raised to $7,200), regional directors got $3,600, and state directors, $2,500 to $3,000.

What's important to remember about the $23.86 salary is that on an annual basis, most actors earned more than they ever did in the commercial theater. And they knew they would work every week. It was a job security they had never before enjoyed.

Job security was just one of the goals of the WPA and

its chief, Harry Hopkins. When FDR was governor of New York, this small-town Iowan had directed relief for the state. Hopkins was a most unconventional social worker. One diplomat said of him, "He had the purity of St. Francis of Assisi combined with the sharp shrewdness of a race track tout." (Hopkins loved to play the horses.) A beanpole of a man, sallow as a poolhall lizard, he was outspoken and often rude. His speech was full of expletives and wisecracks. He drank gallons of coffee and smoked cartons of cigarettes per day.

Given the enormous task of putting millions of hungry people to work at once, Hopkins mastered spending millions per hour. Inevitably, he was accused of being a "waster," an irresponsible spender. In his four and a half years as head of federal relief, he was the target of more attacks than all the other New Dealers combined. But what I, and millions more who were helped through the WPA, remember him for, is his humanity. "Work relief costs more than direct relief," he said, "but the cost is justified. First, in the saving of morale. Second, in the preservation of human skills and talents. Third, in the material enrichment which the unemployed add to our national wealth through their labors."

Hopkins had studied enough history to know that the question of government's relation to the individual was not a new one. Way back, he said, the government had started doing things for people. Out of the national domain, it had given free land to veterans and other settlers. It had given vast tracts to railroad builders to help span the continent. It had spent fortunes for public improvement of roads, canals, waterways, and harbors. It had subsidized struggling industries by imposing protective tariffs. It had given franchises to public utilities, created credit for banks, given patent protection to inventors. Why, then, shouldn't the government use money from its treasury to put the unemployed to work at projects useful to the nation?

Hopkins insisted that unemployed people in the arts must eat and work. Within a few months, the WPA had more than 38,000 of us engaged in programs designed for our needs and capacities. Out of the $5 billion Congress allotted for emergency relief, $27 million was funneled into what was called Federal Project Number One. Its aim was not only to provide work, but to satisfy the hunger of America's millions for plays, books, music, and pictures. It did this through four organizations—the Federal Art, Music, Theatre, and Writers Projects.

Some people asked, Why help the artists? Pay them, instead, to use a shovel or a rake. Aubrey Williams, a WPA administrator, had an answer: "We don't think a good musician should be asked to turn second-rate laborer in order that a sewer may be laid for relative permanency rather than a concert given for the momentary pleasure of our people."

This was a revolutionary idea, coming from a public official. The making of concertos, plays, novels, poems, paintings, and sculpture was not "work" in the minds of most people. These activities were luxuries for the rich to toy with, or avocations for people who worked at "regular" jobs. The arts were not considered part of popular education and culture. And politicians who appealed for votes did little or nothing to change this way of thinking. Yet now, in the middle of the Great Depression, we were beginning to learn something that we should have known long ago: Art was a necessity, something everybody's spirit thirsted for.

The New Deal had been willing to help artists even before the establishment of the WPA. In its very first year the New Deal had given relief funds to the Treasury De-

partment to set up the Public Works of Art Project
(PWAP). This was the idea of George Biddle, an artist
and a friend of the Roosevelt family. PWAP hired painters
and sculptors to embellish public buildings. Its criterion
for hiring was recognized competence, *not* economic need.
But the organizations of artists and writers that sprang up
early in the Depression criticized the government for paying salaries to affluent artists rather than to hungry ones.
Still, PWAP was a pioneering step. It set a precedent for
government support of a national arts project.

At the same time, two relief agencies that preceded the
WPA were subsidizing small projects for needy writers and
musicians in several states. These also helped to pave the
way for the WPA. It took steady pressure from organized
artists, however, to bring Federal One to birth. The Authors
Guild and the fledgling Newspaper Guild were among the
many professional groups that urged the New Deal to
create a national work project for unemployed writers.
They were joined by two new radical groups, the Writers
Union and the Unemployed Writers Association.

The big problem in Washington was setting up the
structure for the arts projects, developing programs, and
putting people to work. Headquarters in the 1890s McLean
mansion at DuPont Circle housed all four arts projects.
They were under the aegis of Jacob Baker, chief of the
WPA's white-collar division. He had been a teacher, a
mine superintendent, a personnel expert, and a book publisher. Here, the men and women who had been chosen to
head the various projects gathered to discuss their plans
with Hopkins and Baker. Nikolai Sokoloff was to head the
music project; Hallie Flanagan, theater; Henry Alsberg,
writers; and Holger Cahill, art. These—the Big Four—
had their own enthusiasms for the marvelous possibilities
opened up by the WPA. At one session with Hopkins,

The jobless lined up on the street for free soup or bread in the early days of the Depression. They were always men; the hungry women stayed away. *United States Information Agency, Photo No. 306-NT-165-3193 in the National Archives*

Ralph Ellison. *Gordon Parks*

John Cheever. *The New York Library Picture Collection*

Richard Wright. *The Schomberg Collection*

Saul Bellow. *Jill Krementz*

Berenice Abbott. *Culver Pictures*

Cahill talked about building a national network of community art centers. Alsberg wanted his writers to create richly detailed guidebooks for every state in the Union. Flanagan planned to bring her productions to small towns where living theater had never come. And Sokoloff was convinced that new symphony orchestras could be built in scores of cities throughout the nation.

"When can you get to work?" was Harry Hopkins' response.

In the mind of each director was the question, "How will I do this impossible job?"

How could you create a vital theater with an organization set up primarily for relief? How could you release the energy of artists to do their best work in the midst of a bureaucracy tripping over political hurdles? The conflict among art, politics, and relief was central.

The first months went into the planning and preparation of each project. The time taken should have been longer, but you couldn't delay when hungry actors, musicians, writers, and painters were begging for jobs. There was never enough time to wait for the best idea, to develop the clearest vision, to blueprint the last detail.

Out of the general policy shaped by Hopkins, Baker, and the Big Four, a structure was arrived at. Regional directors supervised the local administration in each state where projects were established. The hope was to reverse the established trend—the centralization of artists in a few metropolitan centers. The goal was to make art the possession of people everywhere.

The leaders of the projects began their work in the hope that it could be outside of politics. What did politicians have to do with their vision of a federal arts program? Everything, as they soon found out. The program could begin and continue only if the WPA could get the necessary funds from Congress. And Congress was made up of politicians. Southern conservatives, especially, by virtue of their long seniority, held the key posts on committees. They controlled the purse. If the WPA did anything that displeased the men in power, the projects risked being crippled or destroyed.

The press, heavily Republican in the thirties, opposed the WPA concept of work relief. It saw that the WPA's weakest point—and the best target for attack—was the arts program. For the duration of the projects, the press and politicians ridiculed and misrepresented the arts projects. It was easy to appeal to popular ignorance of art and popular suspicion of artists. The mistakes, the weaknesses —and they were many in so hastily conceived and inadequately managed a program—were singled out for laughter and scorn. The effect was to nurture public contempt for the cultural projects.

Hopkins and many of those below him swiftly learned to respect political reality. If they were slow or reluctant to accommodate, they ended up outside. The lesson can be simply stated: The test of a government-sponsored program is not how good it is for the people. It is the degree of support it can win from the people. It would make little difference if famous artists and musicians like Picasso or Toscanini said the Federal Art and Music Projects were important. Or if the country's leading literary critics agreed that the WPA guidebooks were all masterpieces. What counted in the long run was what the people themselves thought of a project's value to *them*, and whether or not they would fight for its political survival.

4 A THEATER THAT TAKES CHANCES

Among artists in the thirties it was theater people who were the worst off by far. The professional theater functions as a group. The play's the thing. And it takes money —a lot of it—to stage a production. Even before the crash, the theater suffered from the rise of sound films and radio.

Before the Depression, my home town, Worcester, had had a stock company that played through the fall and into the spring. They did shows a season or two after they were hits on Broadway. And every once in a while a road company stopped for a few days and gave us the chance to see a star perform. There was vaudeville at two theaters, and burlesque at a third. With the Depression, fewer people could afford the $2.20 or $1.10 commercial theaters had to charge to meet high costs.

By 1932, when I left for New York to attend college, the theater had almost vanished from Worcester. In its place were eight houses showing sound films at prices the theater was never able to match. Going to the movies in the afternoon cost 15 cents, at night a quarter, and kids could always get in for a dime.

The people of the theater could find few jobs. They had to turn to charity. Under pressure from Actors Equity, a few hundred were paid out of relief funds to give free vaudeville, marionette, and legitimate shows in New York. But that was no solution.

It was Hallie Flanagan, more than any other single person, who created a theater program for the WPA. She and Harry Hopkins had been raised and educated in Grinnell, Iowa. As founder and head of the Vassar College Experimental Theatre, she had built a reputation for the superb quality of her productions. The plays she chose were innovative and challenging. One of her own, *Can You Hear Their Voices?*, was a pioneer documentary, dramatizing the plight of farmers devastated by the terrible Arkansas drought. When it played across the country, its power moved audiences to political action.

Such theater was not typical of Broadway. In Flanagan's eyes, the commercial theater had twisted a struggling art into a cold gamble for profit. With thousands of idle actors hanging around Hollywood hoping for a movie job, the legitimate theater had shrunk to a commercial enterprise confined to ten blocks around Times Square. An early thirties study showed that half the theaters in New York were closed, over half the actors were unemployed, and a third of the productions were revivals of old hits.

Beyond the bounds of the commercial Broadway theater was another kind. Like Flanagan's at Vassar College, there were community or university theaters staffed by graduates trained in the drama. They had sunk roots in their region and had become healthy artistic and social influences. Hallie Flanagan hoped that these would one day grow into a permanent national theater. Not an elegant marble temple to theater erected in the capital—no, she wanted the Federal Theatre Project to work "toward an art in which each region and eventually each state would have its unique, indigenous dramatic expression, its company housed in a building reflecting its own landscape and regional materials, producing plays of its past and present, in its own rhythm of speech and its native design, in an essentially American pattern."

She was an unknown on Broadway, but that was a good reason for Hopkins to make her his choice to head the Federal Theatre Project. The Roosevelts, whose home was nearby at Hyde Park, knew her theater work at Vassar. When she came to Washington (she was forty-five then) to discuss her new job, Eleanor Roosevelt told her she hoped "the time had come when Americans might consider the theatre, as it was considered abroad, a part of education."

Flanagan knew a great deal about theater abroad. The first woman to be awarded a Guggenheim Fellowship, she had spent a year studying theater wherever it flourished in Europe, including Soviet Russia. On her return, she had written a book about it. Out of such experience came her vision of the Federal Theatre Project.

John Houseman, who later became an influential producer, director, and actor in theater and film, worked for her on the WPA. To him she was "a wild little woman," a "dreamer and experimenter," a "fanatic" with heretical ideas. At his first meeting with her, she struck him as "a small, forthright, enthusiastic lady with strong teeth, whose matted red hair lay like a wig on her skull and who seemed to take her vast responsibilities with amazing self-confidence and sang-froid."

She wanted the Federal Theatre Project to give its audiences plays dealing with contemporary issues, plays stressing regional themes. Flanagan encouraged experiment in the use of musical comedy, vaudeville, circus. She hoped to develop theater for children. The WPA project, she said, must be "national in scope, regional in emphasis, and democratic in allowing each local unit freedom."

In the theater, as in the other arts projects, art and relief clashed when hiring took place. What was a "professional"? The question worried the directors of the various projects. It was almost impossible to define a professional actor, painter, writer, or musician. As Robert Cronbach, a sculptor on the WPA, pointed out:

> Various elements—professional training, professional experience, ability to earn one's living in this profession, public or professional recognition—all these enter in. But almost immediately one can think of many great artists who would lack one or more, sometimes all, of these qualifications. And conversely, one can call to mind many thoroughly qualified mediocrities. Nevertheless, the weakness of this key definition did not prove a major obstacle to setting up an art project.

In my own case, I had only the flimsiest claim to professionalism as a writer. I was simply too young then to have gathered the necessary experience or recognition. The same was true of many needy young people who were taken on the projects to work side by side with far more experienced talent. I know we youthful apprentices learned from our elders, and perhaps our elders also acquired something from our innocence and eagerness to try the unknown.

"Is this social work or theatre?" one director moaned in a letter to project headquarters. He was wrestling with this mixture of "capables" and "incapables." When payroll cuts had to be made, it was often the less capable who went first. But those who remained were retrained. Out of

their backgrounds and skills Hallie Flanagan used imagi-
nation and ingenuity to create artistic productions that
often earned warm responses from audiences.

But providing busywork for needy actors was not her
purpose. Flanagan wanted to create new audiences by presenting the plays of new dramatists. She was sure Americans would welcome a "free, adult, uncensored theatre"
grappling with the economic and social issues of modern
life, experimenting with new forms and techniques.

To encourage the writing of drama, the Federal Theatre
Project started a playwrights' unit in New York. Into it
went about a dozen young men and women, all on relief
and eager to learn to write plays. They were placed under
the wing of Howard Koch, who would one day write that
immortal movie *Casablanca*—among many other films and
plays. In 1935, Koch was "an extremely tall, spindly,
hollow-eyed, earnest young man." That was how John
Houseman described him. Koch had practiced law briefly,
disliked it, and quit to write plays. One of his plays was
produced. Though not a success on Broadway, it did well
on the road. It was a small reputation, but enough to win
Hallie Flanagan's confidence. This is how the playwrights'
unit operated, said Koch:

To get into the group people had to submit an acceptable piece of work—story, sketch, draft of a play. About
once a week they'd show me what they were working
on, and we'd discuss it in my office. Usually these were
private sessions, occasionally it was group criticism. If
a writer had run out of ideas for what to do next, we'd
try to come up with something useful. We all met off
the Project, too, eating, drinking, talking shop at my
place or one of theirs. The main thing was to encourage
them to develop. When a finished draft was submitted

the final word wasn't mine, but Elmer Rice's [then the head of the New York project], and later his successor's, Philip Barber.

Hallie Flanagan encouraged everyone to write plays on American historical themes. I remember one of our group worked on General Custer, taking a critical view of that military hero. A few of the units' plays were produced by WPA, but to my knowledge, only one or two of the writers made any mark later on. One was Ellis St. Joseph, who became a film writer of quality. But then, he came to us with published stories, and reading them you knew at once he had talent.

It was like most schools of writing: the talented came through no matter what the teacher did.

This was true in Koch's case, too. Just before joining the WPA he had finished a play, *The Lonely Man*, about a reincarnated Lincoln who discovers, seventy years after Emancipation, that black people are still not free in America. The Federal Theatre produced the play in Chicago, with the young John Huston playing Lincoln's role. (Later, Huston would become one of Hollywood's leading directors, responsible for *The Maltese Falcon* and *Treasure of the Sierra Madre*.) It ran for six months. Koch finally left the WPA to write for the Mercury Theatre of the Air. His radio script, "The Men from Mars," made such a terrifying sensation it brought him the Hollywood offer most writers yearned for. Especially during the Depression.

Flanagan insisted the Federal Theatre should not concern itself with politics or specific political candidates. But what dominated the thirties was a struggle to realize a better life. That, surely, was the theater's business. Plays could deal with any social theme, Flanagan believed, so long as they were good theater. In such a turbulent time, when everyone was searching out the roots of what was wrong, playwrights were bound to tackle social issues.

The Federal Theatre Project produced many such works. There was *Class of '29* (Orrie Lashin and Milo Hastings), telling the story of four college graduates launched on the tidal wave of the Depression. And *Chalk Dust* (Harold H. Clarke and Maxwell Nurnberg), attacking bureaucracy and intolerance in big-city high schools. *Altars of Steel* (Thomas Hall-Rogers) pictured the exploitation of the South by the steel industry. *Life and Death of an American* (George Sklar) dealt with the hero's struggle for "the right to live as a decent human being." Many plays used historical parallels to the day's issues as a springboard. *Battle Hymn* (Michael Gold and Michael Blankfort) was the story of John Brown's fight against injustice to blacks, and *The Sun and I* (Barrie and Leona Stavis) went back to the Egypt of the pharaohs to portray the dictatorships of ancient Mussolinis and Hitlers.

New York City, long the center of the nation's commercial theater, was naturally the largest section of the project. In its first year of life it created four major productions which proved the Federal Theatre's worth. *Chalk Dust* was one of them. A sensational *Macbeth* was another. The brilliant adaptation of Shakespeare was the work of two men. John Houseman produced the play for the WPA Negro Theatre in Harlem, and Orson Welles, then only twenty, directed it. They placed it in a Haitian setting. The critics hailed it as "spectacular" and "magnificent." It was a huge success.

Far different from *Macbeth* was the equally successful production of T. S. Eliot's *Murder in the Cathedral*. It discussed the conflict between church and state through the story of the martyrdom of Thomas à Becket. Here the

WPA took a great chance. It had been acclaimed in London as the most important play in verse in a generation, but Broadway refused to gamble on such a poetic work. This was precisely the kind of risk Hallie Flanagan felt the Federal Theatre should take. Its staging of the difficult poetic drama was called by *The New York Times* critic, "a severely beautiful production worthy of the stinging verse of its author . . . a moving and triumphant performance." In the leading role of Becket was the actor Harry Irvine, who had been dropped by Broadway because his hands shook. "Too old to work" was their verdict. But *Newsweek's* critic said, "If the Federal Theatre Project can put on something like *Murder in the Cathedral* better for 55 cents than a professional manager subsequently proves he can for $3.30, then—much as it pains me to say it—the hell with the professional managers."

The fourth hit of that first Federal Theatre season was *Triple-A Plowed Under*, presented by the Living Newspaper. No unit of the project was to be more praised or more damned.

5 THE LIVING NEWSPAPER VERSUS THE DEADLY CENSOR

With the stage dark, the Voice of the Living Newspaper announces over a loudspeaker: "Summer, 1934. Drought sears the Midwest, West, and Southwest."

A spotlight picks up a farmer kneeling in his parched field. Two voices are heard alternately over the loudspeaker. In staccato tones the first announces, "May first, Midwest weather report." The second, a foreboding voice, replies, "Fair and warmer." As the forecast is repeated for May 2, 3, and 4, the music grows more intense. The farmer who is examining his soil straightens up, and the music reaches a pitch of intense despair. He stands, slowly letting a handful of the parched and useless soil sift through his fingers, and cries out, "Dust!"

That is a scene from the Living Newspaper, *Triple-A Plowed Under*. It is based on facts, documented facts, but something more—emotion—and is more effective onstage than in the telling. Swiftly the Living Newspaper moved, with one brief sketch following another, unfolding the farm problem as it grew worse from the twenties on into the thirties. The audience saw land devastated by drought, mortgages foreclosed, farms auctioned off or deliberately destroyed, and the middleman raking in excessive profits. They watched farmer and consumer joining in cooperatives, they sat in on the creation of the New Deal farm agency, the Agricultural Adjustment Administration (AAA). Then they heard the Supreme Court declare the AAA unconstitutional. They listened to debate in Congress over the farmer's fate. And they heard the news that here and there farmers and workers were uniting to shape their own future.

The Living Newspaper, as its name implies, was a form of reporting—but not a literal record of facts. The artist imposed form through selection, argument, emphasis, point of view. The effectiveness of the Living Newspaper was achieved by careful editing and full use of technical resources. The information and evidence were gathered painstakingly by research and were given a conscious, theatrical design—in the case of *Triple-A*, by the Living Newspaper staff, not by a single playwright.

Whose idea was it to dramatize the news with living actors, light, music, movement? There have been many claims, but no one knows when or where the original idea was born. Flanagan had already tried it out at Vassar with her *Can You Hear Their Voices?*

The impulse this time came from the necessity to find ways to put great numbers of actors to work. Most plays use small casts, and even twenty productions done at once would employ far too few WPA actors. So the Federal Theatre Project decided to set up the Living Newspaper unit. It secured the sponsorship of the Newspaper Guild, and from its leaders chose Morris Watson to head the unit.

Functioning like a big-city daily, the Living Newspaper staff (many drawn from journalists on relief) ransacked newspaper files, magazines, books, and government reports to find the facts upon which to construct a dramatic treatment of current issues. It was not the event that was dramatized, but the problem. The idea was to show the importance of a news event to the people it affected.

Through the Living Newspaper, wrote an historian of the stage, John Gassner, the Federal Theatre "gave rise to the one original form of drama developed in the United States."

What was original about it? According to Gassner:

The Living Newspaper style can be described as an amalgam of motion-picture, epic theatre, commedia dell' arte, and American minstrel show techniques kept within the framework of a question asked, usually by a puzzled little man who represents the public, and answers supplied by a series of presentational devices consisting of scenes, demonstrations, slides, lectures, and arguments. Symbolism was not excluded from this technique. . . . Pageantry was also not foreign to the medium. . . . Naturalism could also be assimilated into the medium, when this was deemed theatrically feasible.

This was one of the Federal Theatre's aims, as Flanagan put it: "To dramatize a new struggle—the search of the average American today for knowledge about his country and his world; to dramatize his struggle to turn the great natural and economic and social forces of our time toward a better life for more people."

Take *Triple-A Plowed Under*, the unit's first success. It tackled the plight of the farmer, tracing its history and the effect upon the people at large. It used news, history and economics, graph and cartoon, screen and chorus, blackout and film slides. It introduced the loudspeaker as commentator—the Voice of the Living Newspaper. Arthur Arent, chief writer for the unit, said of this device:

> It spoke lines, it editorialized, it became a definite character, but never the same for long. It was at various times in the same play ignorant, thirsting for information, and a veritable Britannica of esoteric facts and statistics; it became helpful and sympathetic at one moment, bellicose, disdainful and sly at others. In short, it was all things to all men, and particularly to the dramatist.

A short scene from *Triple-A* shows the ingenuity with which a bare news item was made powerfully human. In this rich but Depression-torn land, farmers were unable to make a living growing crops, while people in the cities starved. The researchers clipped a story from the New York *Daily News* about a Mrs. Dorothy Sherwood who had just gone on trial for drowning her infant son. Here is her statement, exactly as printed in the *News*:

> She [Mrs. Sherwood] walked into the Police Court with the baby in her arms and said, "He's dead, I just drowned my son because I couldn't feed him and I couldn't bear to see him hungry. . . . I let him wade in the creek until he got tired. Then I led him out into the middle and held him there until he stopped moving. I had only five cents and he was hungry. . . . I just thought it had to be done, that's all."

Here is the news item transformed into a scene played on the stage of the theater:

LOUDSPEAKER: Newburgh, New York, August 20th, 1935. . . . Mrs. Dorothy Sherwood . . .

(*Overhead spot picks out police desk, down right. Behind it, a* LIEUTENANT. *Enter,* MRS. SHERWOOD, *left, with her dead infant in her arms. She walks to desk, follow spot on her.*)

MRS. SHERWOOD (*stops at desk*): He's dead, I drowned him.

LIEUTENANT: You *what?*

MRS. SHERWOOD: I just drowned my son, I couldn't feed him and I couldn't bear to see him hungry. . . . I let him wade in the creek until he got tired. Then I led him out into the middle and held him there until he stopped moving.

LIEUTENANT (*calling, not too loudly*): John!

(POLICEMAN *enters lighted area*). Take the body. Book this woman for murder.

(*Black out everything; music; a solitary spot picks out* MRS. SHERWOOD, *center, facing out.*)

OFFSTAGE VOICE (*amplified*): Why did you do it?

MRS. SHERWOOD: I couldn't feed him. I only had five cents.

VOICE: Your own child! Did you think you were doing the right thing?

MRS. SHERWOOD: I just thought it had to be done, that's all.

VOICE: How could a mother kill her own child?

MRS. SHERWOOD: He was hungry, I tell you. Hungry, hungry, hungry!

(*As her voice mounts, it is blended with that of another, the first in a progression of twelve voices crying, "Guilty!" These, amplified and varying in color, increase in fervor until. . . .*)

Dimout

Such an innovative, experimental production puzzled and dismayed many of the actors. During rehearsals they complained that there was no story, no plot, no chance to build up a character. And what did New York audiences care about farmers and grain prices?

Flanagan and Joseph Losey, *Triple-A*'s director, had to persuade the cast that the Federal Theatre must take chances on the new if it was to succeed. The WPA was not out to compete with Broadway, but to create something audiences could not get elsewhere. Trust us, they pleaded. If the play fails, we'll drop the Living Newspaper idea. The response of audience and critics on opening night was so enthusiastic that the actors became zealous converts to this new dramatic form.

Highlights of 1935 was next. It was a kaleidoscopic report of the year's events. Then *Injunction Granted*, dealing with labor's right to organize. Both were written collectively by the staff. After that, *Power*, by Arthur Arent, which took up the relationship between the consumer and the electric utility companies. It had thirty-three scenes and used eighty-eight actors. Before it opened, 60,000 New Yorkers, delighted with the earlier Living Newspapers, had bought tickets.

Solidly grounded in annotated sources, *Power* was called by *The New York Times* critic "the most indignant and militant proletarian drama of the season." To *Life*'s reviewer it was "exciting and unique" propaganda for government ownership of electric power.

When the final curtain came down on opening night, Harry Hopkins went backstage to meet the cast. "I want to tell you," he said, "this is a great show. It's fast and funny, it makes you laugh and it makes you cry and it makes you think—I don't know what more anyone can ask of a show. I want this play and plays like it done from one end of the country to the other."

Then he anticipated the attacks: "People will say it's propaganda. Well, I say what of it? It's propaganda to educate the consumer who's paying for power. It's about time someone had some propaganda for him. The big power companies have spent millions on propaganda for the utilities. It's about time the consumer had a mouthpiece. I say, more plays like *Power* and more power to you."

A year later, *One-Third of a Nation* opened. Written by Arthur Arent, it was a Living Newspaper indictment of the degradation of the slums. It was first tried out at a national summer workshop for Federal Theatre staff. When the curtain went up, the audience saw a huge garbage can, a cracked toilet seat, a rusty water tap, and an old-law fire escape dangling from the flies. It was the idea of Howard Bay, a young WPA designer. Bay believed the ultrarealism of the movies made stage realism thin and pallid. Like a surrealist painter, he placed these everyday objects of the slums in an extraordinary framework that would assault the senses. Toilet seat and garbage can were facts of life but now, under Abe Feder's ingenious lighting, they became symbols. Here was their true significance, the epitome of slum squalor.

When *One-Third of a Nation* opened in New York early in 1938, the press called it the Federal Theatre's most important contribution. For the New York production, Howard Bay had created onstage a four-story cross section of a slum tenement. The set itself became an evil force in the action. The play ended with the burning of the tenement, a nightly feature that horrified and stirred the audience. A quarter of a million people saw the New York production directed by Lem Ward. Revised to portray local housing conditions, *One-Third* was staged in many cities—Detroit, Cincinnati, New Orleans, Hartford, Philadelphia, Seattle, and Portland.

"No lecture on the slums," wrote one critic, "has ever been half so graphic and horrific." A New Orleans paper called the local version "a dramatic bombshell" offering the city "a startled initiation into the roaring effectiveness of a new stage medium."

Chicago's Federal Theatre developed its own Living Newspaper and made a daring choice of subject—syphilis. Called *Spirochete*, it described what venereal disease has done to man throughout history and how man has tried to cope with it. It took a great deal of courage in the thirties to present any subject dealing with sex. But the medical profession and the press, aware of how desperately ignorant the public was, welcomed the attempt. Written by Arnold Sundgaard, a young WPA dramatist, the production earned applause for its educational power and its "superb staging and lighting."

There were many other attempts by Federal Theatre units to produce Living Newspapers. In Iowa, *Dirt* was to dramatize the land question and soil conservation; in Denver, there was *Sugar*; in Seattle, *Timber*; in California, *Spanish Grant*; in Oregon, *Bonneville Dam*. Unfortunately, none of these saw an opening night. Because so many of the projects were shut down, the plays were never performed.

Could a government-supported theater investigate such social issues without the fear of censorship? It would have been foolish to think so. *One-Third of a Nation* was called by *The New York Times* critic "a rabble-rouser of uncommon eloquence, a caustic and vibrant piece of theatrical muckraking." One of its brief scenes documented the

Senate debate over a federal housing bill. A few Southern senators (Democrats) who had some reservations about the bill were accurately quoted. But they complained to WPA headquarters that they were being held up to ridicule and made to appear the villains by a project funded out of the public treasury. Flanagan denied the charges and said such criticism was only a tribute to the power of the theater to reform.

Censorship was a threat to the project from the beginning. *Ethiopia*, the very first Living Newspaper, was intended to dramatize the rape of that country by Italy. Mussolini, the Fascist ruler of Italy, had sent his troops into Africa to conquer Haile Selassie's kingdom. When the White House heard the Living Newspaper wished to use a radio broadcast by FDR along with speeches by Mussolini and Haile Selassie, it protested. Impersonating the heads of state onstage in a federal project would be harmful. Even quoting their words via loudspeaker would endanger foreign relations, the White House said. After much argument over the issue, the New York director of the project, playwright Elmer Rice, resigned. He was convinced the Democratic administration was scared to tackle controversial issues of any kind for fear of offending the powerful Southern wing of the party. *Ethiopia* was scrapped. But Hallie Flanagan did not intend to lose any more rounds. She would hold Harry Hopkins to his promise of "a free, adult, uncensored theater."

But even the seemingly "safe" play could offend some congressman or other. *Prologue to Glory*, E. P. Conkle's story of the young Lincoln, was attacked by Congressman J. Parnell Thomas. He said the drama showed "Honest Abe" doing battle with politicians. What was it, then, but "a propaganda play to prove all politicians are crooked"? In this case, Thomas had a right to feel nervous. Years later he was sentenced to prison for being a crooked politician.

The most explosive example of censorship occurred in the early summer of 1937. While the air was full of alarming rumors about massive cuts on WPA, the Federal Theatre in New York was rehearsing *The Cradle Will Rock*. Set in Steeltown, USA, it was a hard-driving contemporary opera, witty and acid as a Daumier cartoon. Its theme was corruption, the sellout of talent and dignity to the powerful. Words and music were by Marc Blitzstein, a thirty-one-year-old Philadelphian whose father was a banker and a socialist. Blitzstein was a serious composer of modern music. He wrote *Cradle* in five weeks and dedicated it to Bertolt Brecht, an anti-Nazi writer forced to flee Hitler Germany. Brecht had developed new forms of theater which influenced Blitzstein.

At that time the steel industry was under siege by the newly formed Congress of Industrial Organizations (CIO), and several of the companies were putting up violent resistance to unionization. Blitzstein turned to cops and capitalists and union organizers for his characters, and took the action into night court, drugstore, hotel lobby, faculty lounge, street corner, and salvation mission. His style was a mixture of realism, vaudeville, and oratory. Blitzstein gave the man on the street a musical voice—the first serious attempt to do this in American musical drama. It was superb theater, but it was also political dynamite. Flanagan did not hesitate to approve its production. The young producer-director team of John Houseman and Orson Welles, who had triumphed with their *Macbeth*, took charge. They cast Will Geer and Howard da Silva in the leading parts. (Geer later became a film actor and in the seventies played the role of "Grandpa" in the highly rated television series, *The Waltons*. Da Silva starred in many roles in the theater, movies, and television.)

Trouble again. Washington thought it was too dangerous a show to do at a time when the battle to organize steel was in the daily headlines and the WPA itself was threatened with drastic cuts. The press was saying *Cradle* would take labor's side. With 18,000 advance tickets sold, and *Cradle* ready to open in June, Flanagan got word from Washington that no new productions could take place until after July 1. The official reason given was that cuts in project personnel had to be made and the Federal Theatre reorganized before new shows could open.

"This was obviously censorship under a different guise," Flanagan wrote later. She tried in vain to get an exception made for *Cradle*. Then Orson Welles flew to the capital to convince the WPA that the play was "not a political protest but an artistic one." When he threatened to produce *Cradle* with private funds, the WPA administrator, undoubtedly relieved, said, "Go ahead."

Two nights later, a benefit preview audience was standing before the locked doors of the WPA's theater on Thirty-ninth Street. NO SHOW TONIGHT, read the handlettered sign tacked up on the door. Inside, WPA guards stood over scenery, costumes, props, and lights, instructed to prevent their unauthorized use. Welles and Houseman moved through the agitated crowd outside, assuring them that somehow the show would go on. But the musicians' and the actors' unions had forbidden their members to appear onstage for any management but the Federal Theatre.

Where could they perform, then? And how?

An hour before curtain time, the miracle happened. Someone made a deal to open the dark and dingy old

Venice Theatre on Seventh Avenue at Fifty-eighth Street.
The announcement was made to the crowd that curtain
time would be at 9:00 P.M.—a mile uptown. By subway,
bus, taxi, and on foot, the audience, sensing it was part
of an historic moment, headed north. Some of the cast and
chorus dropped away, fearful of losing their bread money
for defying their unions and the WPA.

The crowd, through word-of-mouth swollen to 2,000
now, poured into the big theater, filling it to the last seat.
There was no one to take tickets or to usher.

Houseman and Welles stepped in front of the curtain
to explain what had caused this strange event, and why
they were defying the WPA order. Then the curtain went
up. There, alone on the stage, sat the nervous Marc Blitzstein in his shirtsleeves at an untuned, old upright piano—
its front pulled out for greater volume. The spotlight on
him, he spoke to set the scene, "A streetcorner: Steeltown,
USA."

From the lower left box in the audience, a quavery
soprano voice floated out over the crowd. Startled, the
audience turned, following a spotlight. Out of the darkness
it picked up a slender girl in a green dress. With every
note, her frightened voice grew stronger. The other actors
took courage from Olive Stanton. None of them had
known what he or she would do in this crisis. As her last
note ended, a young man down in the orchestra stood up
and spoke his lines to the girl in the box. Now the audience
realized: The actors, to avoid violating their union's ban,
had scattered throughout the theater. They. had been forbidden to perform onstage, and they were everywhere but
onstage.

The spotlight swung to the Reverend Salvation, then to
Mr. Mister, Steeltown's tyrant, then to Larry Foreman, the
union organizer. One after another, actors rose to sing

their parts, accompanied by the composer at his piano. It was a night I'll never forget. I was part of that lucky audience which shared a thrilling moment of theater history. The morning papers gave front-page stories to "the runaway opera."

This sensational event cut short the Houseman-Welles career on the WPA. But *The Cradle Will Rock* launched a new venture for them, their Mercury Theatre. Since the thirties, *Cradle* has been produced many times. For American theater it became as historic a creation as the Kurt Weill–Bertolt Brecht *Threepenny Opera* was for German theater.

The *Cradle* episode, dramatic as it was, was only one of several attempts at censorship. Later, in California, a production of Elmer Rice's *Judgment Day* was canceled. The play dealt with a trial in an unnamed totalitarian state and pictured the corruption and oppression suffered under a dictatorship. The order to stop the production came from a state WPA administrator, one of the many army officers now staffing key WPA posts. As with most of the others, he behaved like an autocrat. Despite a nationwide protest over his decision, the WPA headquarters in Washington insisted it was not a case of censorship, only a matter of "selection."

The issue of *Judgment Day* came up again when the national directors of the four arts projects met in Washington. They joined together to protest censorship and demanded that the directors of the arts projects retain artistic control of program and personnel. When they threatened to resign unless supported, they won. *Judgment Day* was allowed to open.

Perhaps it was such victories that made Flanagan optimistic about the future of government-sponsored theater. In her book *Arena* she wrote:

Censorship, although an ever-present danger, emanated more from local than from national WPA officials. In spite of the censorship cases which did occur, our experience proved that if great care is exercised in selection of plays it is possible to operate under our democratic form of government a theatre which is more free from censorship than any government-sponsored theatre in any other country.

Note that Flanagan did not claim a federal theater in the United States could be totally free of censorship, simply "more free" than elsewhere—and she had seen such theaters all over Europe.

In his study of *Federal Relief Administration and the Arts*, Professor William F. McDonald of Ohio State University made this point about censorship on the WPA:

No congressman ever suggested that a *private* producer should be denied the right to produce a play presenting a particular social philosophy, or criticizing the government or members of Congress. The question was whether a governmental agency, supported by public funds, should produce a play presenting a social philosophy with which at least a substantial minority of the population was not in sympathy. Certainly, if a Republican administration operating a theatre project should have produced a play extolling private monopoly, those who were opposed to that philosophy would have protested no less vigorously. This is only another way of saying that so long as there exists in a democratic commonwealth a substantial minority opposed to the philosophy of the party in power, an uncensored governmental theatre is a precarious undertaking.

6 SHAW AND O'NEILL: 55 CENTS

The Federal Theatre's greatest hope was to become a truly national theater. Its leaders struggled against terrible odds to achieve that goal, but they never made it. At its peak, 13,000 people worked in theater units scattered over thirty-one states. Yet the regional centers Flanagan dreamed of could not be built. Many places lacked the necessary local talent. And the changing political fortunes of WPA crippled long-range planning.

The next best thing was to send touring companies out on the road. But the complex arrangements required, the doubled costs of traveling with a show, the delays in finding local sponsorship, and the inevitable conflicts of authority made national or even regional tours almost impossible.

In spite of all that, theater in a dozen different forms was brought to millions of people around the country. Vaudeville companies delighted children in reformatories and orphanages, boys in CCC camps, patients in hospitals. By 1937, there were nearly a hundred vaudeville units in the country. About one-fourth of all Federal Theatre activity

involved vaudeville, and much of its work was free entertainment. These units played at lodges, granges, clubs, and
town councils. When the Ohio River's floodwaters ram-
paged through the river valley, the vaudevillians climbed
into boats and trucks and brought their cheer to the
homeless and forlorn victims of disaster.

Summer was the caravan season. Out under the sky
strolling actors played Shakespeare to thousands of people
in city parks free of charge. If they would or could not
come to the theater, the WPA would bring theater to them.
In the CCC camps young men crowded into mess halls
to see all kinds of plays, including *The CCC Murder
Mystery*. It was such a hit that nine companies toured it
for two years to almost 300 camps. A Gilbert and Sullivan
company developed a repertory of seven operas for the
large number of people devoted to that famous light-
opera team.

Both puppets and marionettes were favored by recrea-
tion centers, schools, and other institutions. One unit, the
Buffalo Historical Marionettes, experimented with visual
education, depicting everything from the lives of composers to the dangers of reckless driving. It played to half
a million people in New York State, mostly children. The
group toured as far south as West Virginia, where 25,000
people blocked traffic to see them. In Peoria, Illinois, a
Federal Theatre unit brought ten shows out to rural audiences. Federal Theatre actors played in college halls and
police stations, in circus tents and on showboats, in
churches and convents—anywhere an audience might
gather.

For black theater workers the WPA provided not only
jobs and security but the broadest chance for professional
growth they had yet known. The middle-class little-theater
groups organized by blacks in the twenties had served up

only warmed-over commercial hits. Even the theaters in black colleges had been timid in their choice of plays— leaning heavily on Shakespeare and the Greek classics. In all its history down to the mid-thirties, the Broadway theater had presented only seven plays by black writers.

Under the Federal Theatre Project, black actors, writers, directors, and technicians found opportunities long denied them. The WPA established black units in New York, Newark, Philadelphia, Boston, Hartford, Chicago, Seattle, San Francisco, Los Angeles, and two in the South— in Raleigh and Birmingham.

They succeeded in pleasing audiences with a great variety of productions. But few dealt with the black strug- gle for equality. Since each unit had to serve the whole community, the stress was more on entertainment than honest portrayal of contemporary black life. As the black writer and critic Sterling Brown observed, audiences sought "escape from drudgery and insult by laughter."

Black artists not content with a diet of comedy, musi- cals, and melodrama criticized the Federal Theatre for not doing more to encourage black playwrights. It made a try. Realizing no serious black theater could develop without black playwrights, the New York project invited a hundred black writers to participate in an extended drama work- shop. About fifty enrolled, and the workshop lasted four months. Out of it came more than twenty plays, two of which were produced by the Federal Theatre and one on Broadway.

New York had the largest black theater unit. It employed 750 people, about 150 of them seasoned professional per- formers. The unit began under joint black-white leadership. Rose McClendon, the distinguished black actress who knew and respected John Houseman's work with black per- formers, recommended him to be her co-director. But she died of cancer six months later, and Houseman was left in sole charge. In its first year at the Lafayette Theatre in Harlem the group offered four plays: Frank Wilson's *Walk Together Chillun*, dealing with a race riot in the North; Rudolph Fisher's *Conjure Man Dies*, a comic whodunit; Peter Morrell and J. A. Smith's *Turpentine*, a protest drama set in the South; and the Haitian version of *Macbeth*.

After a half-year's run, *Macbeth* was sent on a triumphant national tour of WPA theaters. Houseman and Welles left Harlem to establish the new WPA production unit that would soon get entangled with *The Cradle Will Rock*. And Gus Smith and Carlton Moss took leadership of the black company.

The immediate benefits of the Federal Theatre to blacks were apparent. But any long-range influence is hard to trace. The Federal Theatre did not last long enough to provide the training and experience needed. Not until some thirty years after the WPA's death would black playwrights, actors, and directors create their own theaters.

What Federal Theatre did for children was one of its finest achievements. It set up several units to prepare professional productions exclusively for youngsters. In Los Angeles the Theatre for Youth, headed by Yasha Frank, reached large audiences with its varied repertory. The plays included *Alice in Wonderland, Hansel and Gretel, Pinocchio, Rip Van Winkle*, and *Twelfth Night*. *Pinocchio* made use of fifty retrained vaudevillians in an imaginative musical version of the puppet's story. When it was later presented in New York, its popularity was so great that speculators were getting $6.60 for 55-cent tickets to the WPA show. It became the first children's play to be done on television.

Two Iowans: Hallie Flanagan, head of the Federal Theatre Project, and Harry Hopkins, boss of the WPA. *WPA Photo No. 69-N-1504 in the National Archives*

A scene from Yasha Frank's *Pinocchio*, hit of the WPA Children's Theatre. *WPA Photo No. 69-TGS-33H-3 in the National Archives* (Top)

The spectacular production of *Macbeth* by the Harlem unit of the Federal Theatre was directed by twenty-year-old Orson Welles. *WPA Photo No. 69-TS-22Z-33 in the National Archives* (Right)

Orson Welles (center) in the title role of Marlowe's *The Tragedy of Dr. Faustus*, one of his innovative productions for the Federal Theatre. *WPA Federal Theatre Photos, Municipal Archives of the City of New York*

In the climax of *One-Third of a Nation*, the Living Newspaper's dramatic indictment of slums, the tenement set burst into flames. *WPA Photo No. 69-N-15486C in the National Archives*

One of the children's plays, *The Revolt of the Beavers,* by Oscar Saul and Louis Lantz, dealt with the adventures of two children in Beaverland. A reviewer called it "Marxism à la Mother Goose," which raised a tiny tempest in Congress. But when psychologists tested audience response, they reported the children enjoyed it only as a fairy tale about good and bad beavers.

In Gary, the Indiana steel town, ten adults worked with children of four to eighteen years, who produced plays in their own theater and for other groups, too. The children composed, wrote, danced, acted, and directed their own productions. They presented plays to celebrate the holidays of the city's ethnic groups, as well as classics such as *Robinson Crusoe* and *The Shoemaker and the Elves,* and adaptations of Mark Twain's novels, *The Prince and the Pauper* and *A Connecticut Yankee in King Arthur's Court.* Their audiences ranged from the 150 their own theater could seat to the thousands who came to see them in parks and halls.

Federal Theatre performances in reformatories, hospitals, asylums, and prisons showed how theater could be used as a therapeutic tool. The WPA experience opened new channels for the skills of theater people.

Although it failed to establish regional theaters, the project did play a part in starting the cycle of historical dramas that are now featured in community festivals in many parts of America. The Southern dramatist Paul Green wrote a play about the first English settlers who came to Roanoke Island in 1584 and mysteriously vanished soon after. Joining with state, regional, and university forces, the Federal Theatre produced Green's *Lost Colony* for three summers running. A thousand people made the pilgrimage each week to see the play about the men and women who made our early history. It was the beginning of a tradition that took root, spread, and flourishes today.

The range of plays produced by the WPA was enormous. Besides Shakespeare, the Federal Theatre presented the classics of Aristophanes, Plautus, Lope de Vega, Molière, Jonson, Marlowe, Dekker, Goldsmith, Sheridan, and Schiller. The modern dramatists included Ibsen, Chekhov, Tolstoy, Andreyev, Hauptmann, and Wilde. Among established contemporary writers—both American and European—who received WPA production were Galsworthy, Lady Gregory, O'Casey, Dunsany, Synge, Toller, Molnár, Čapek, Anderson, Wilder, Kaufman, Sherwood, Behrman, Odets, Green, Howard, Connelly, and Barry.

Two of the Western world's greatest playwrights—Eugene O'Neill and George Bernard Shaw—were brought to nationwide audiences by the WPA. Both dramatists had kept tight control of their plays, but the reputation the Federal Theatre built as a people's theater induced O'Neill and Shaw to be generous. Offering his plays for WPA's usual $50 weekly rental rate, Shaw wrote:

> As long as you stick to your fifty-five cent maximum for admission . . . you can play anything of mine you like unless you hear from me to the contrary. . . . Any author of serious plays who does not follow my example does not know what is good for him. I am not making a public-spirited sacrifice; I am jumping at an unprecedentedly good offer.

O'Neill followed at once, under the same arrangement. The Shaw cycle ran to nine of his plays. The Federal Theatre eventually did forty-two productions of fourteen of O'Neill's plays. When Flanagan visited O'Neill at his home in California, and showed the reports on productions of his work in dozens of towns and cities, he said, "This theatre is becoming a great force in the life of American writers and in the history of our stage. It has a tonic effect on me to think of my own plays being done in places where, without Federal Theatre, they would most certainly never have been produced."

How great a force the Federal Theatre could be was shown with the unprecedented nationwide production of a single play. Sinclair Lewis, the Nobel-prizewinning writer, had published an anti-Fascist novel called *It Can't Happen Here*. With Hitler and Mussolini in power in Europe, and Fascistic figures like Huey Long and Father Charles Coughlin wielding great influence in America, Lewis issued his warning that fascism could take over anywhere—even here.

It was the Federal Theatre's own idea to ask Sinclair Lewis to dramatize his novel and to open it all over the country on the same night. This idea multiplied many times the normal difficulties of producing a play on WPA. Nevertheless the play managed to open simultaneously in twenty-one theaters in seventeen states on the night of the Federal Theatre's first anniversary, October 27, 1936.

There were few plays thought to be worth that gigantic effort. But to Flanagan, this one justified it because it was fired by the passionate belief in democracy of one of America's most distinguished writers. Hollywood had refused to film his novel, and Lewis's great enthusiasm for the Federal Theatre made him confident it would do justice to it.

The book's New England setting was varied for each production, so that it would have a local atmosphere to bear out the message that fascism *can* happen anywhere. In Los Angeles and New York's Jewish communities there were also Yiddish productions. In Seattle a black cast did it, and in Tampa, audiences saw a Spanish version.

Although the play was not great drama, it proved to be emotionally powerful because of the temper of the times. Since fascism was not generally favored, the only attacks upon the Federal Theatre for doing "a propaganda play" came from the far right. Audiences flocked to see it month after month. By the time the last curtain came down, the play had run a grand total of 260 weeks, the equivalent of five years.

To Hallie Flanagan there was a special meaning in the grand effort:

> Above all it was significant that hundreds of thousands of people all over America crowded in to see a play which says that when dictatorship threatens a country it does not necessarily come by way of military invasion, that it may arrive in the form of a sudden silencing of free voices. In producing that play the first government-sponsored theatre of the United States was doing what it could to keep alive "the free, inquiring, critical spirit" which is the center and core of a democracy.

7 THE PAINTER
AND THE TIME CLOCK

"Prosperity don't seem to come my way," wrote John Sloan in his diary. "I am too liable to worry when there is no bread and butter coming in." One of the most respected painters in the history of American art, he did not sell a single painting until he was forty-two years old. At fifty, he had sold only six. Today his paintings hang in many major museums.

How did he manage? For sixteen years he supported himself and his wife by drawing puzzles for a Philadelphia newspaper. A gloomy diary entry of 1909 reads, "I take up my old burden of the weekly puzzle which I had hoped was to pass from me, though it is the only steady income I have." A year later, grateful to have it, he wrote, "Finished and mailed the puzzle. The puzzle must be treated respectfully nowadays, as it seems to be our only means of livelihood, good old job!"

Long before the Great Depression, most artists had trouble making a living from their art. Like Sloan, those who could pay the rent and put food on the table did so through all sorts of work, frequently related to their skills

—advertising, illustration, sign painting, lettering, teaching. When the Depression came, it wiped out much of this secondary work that kept artists alive. Axel Horn, a WPA muralist, recalls that some young painters who graduated from art school in the early thirties survived by working on comic books. In those days, they were simply reprints of newspaper comic strips, and artists were paid a tiny amount of money to color them in. The few artists who escaped the necessity of doing commercial work were supported either by their parents or by a spouse with money or a job. But even these lucky ones, it should be remembered, were not surviving on their skills as artists.

It is more than thirty-five years since the Great Depression ended. Are things any different for artists? A recent survey made by the art historian Francis V. O'Connor showed that only 7 percent of the artists who responded to a questionnaire made their entire living from the sale of their art. About 30 percent made more than half their income from their art. But 75 percent had to teach to make ends meet.

Back in the early thirties there were very few ways to make ends meet. Jacob Kainen, the painter and printmaker who later became curator of the Smithsonian Museum, graduated from Pratt Institute in 1930. He tells what happened then:

> I did manage to get a job in a place called the Intaglio Gravure Company. I drew greeting cards in pen and ink. The drawings were reproduced by photogravure. It was fascinating. But of course the job lasted about six months and they went out of business. Then I was absolutely indigent. I lived on relief in a condemned house and paid $10 a month rent. I had an extension cord so I could get electricity through the transom. I

had a heater and lived on beans. . . . It was great to be young, but we had absolutely nothing. No one dreamed of selling a painting. . . .

Or take Jackson Pollock, who became one of the foremost artists of the mid-twentieth century. From 1929 to 1931, he studied at the Art Students League in New York with Thomas Hart Benton, now well known for his American regionalist paintings and murals. One summer Pollock hitchhiked home to California, riding the rails partway. "The freight trains are full of the average American looking for work," he wrote. "Men going west and men going east and as many going north and south—a million of them." For a while Pollock worked as a janitor at the City and Country School in New York. Then, forced to go on relief, to keep himself alive he stole food and fuel from pushcarts in Greenwich Village.

A small group of civic-minded rich people decided to help artists by financing the Gibson Committee. The painter Joseph Solman recalls that back in 1931 the committee sent him, along with several jobless architects, to a farm in New Jersey. In the morning the group did farm labor, and in return they were given the rest of the day to draw, sketch, or paint.

It was local government, working through the College Art Association, that made the next stumbling effort to help artists who were on relief. The files of the association showed that there were over 1,500 artists in New York City who needed help, but were not getting any. As for illustrators, photographers, art researchers, fashion and textile designers, artists' models, and commercial artists— they needed to eat and work, too. New York's mayor agreed to support a small number with $15-a-week wages. Some artists were put to work cleaning statues in the public squares. Jackson Pollock was one of them. The state, too, put up emergency funds. But it was five long years after the Depression set in before the Federal Art Project was created. "A dreadful, dreadful five years," said Audrey McMahon, who, as director of the College Art Association, did so much to get relief for artists:

> All we really did was dole out this tiny little pittance and hope some good would come of it. Then we would try to explain why there was not more and try to get wealthy people to help out the weeks we couldn't. It was a starvation thing. Out of my window I could see people who were working for us sleeping on park benches. That was just how stark things were.

One of the wealthy who conducted a private relief project was Mrs. Gertrude Vanderbilt Whitney, founder of the Whitney Museum in New York. She sent several artists a monthly check of $50. Everyone conspired to keep it a secret.

Shortly after FDR took office, the Treasury Department launched the first of its three government art projects. But it was the WPA that created a national program to embrace all the major visual art forms and activities. In 1935, Holger Cahill was made director of the Federal Art Project. Born on a tenant farm in Minnesota, Cahill had known poverty and unemployment as a youth. At twenty, he came to New York, took courses at the New School for Social Research and at Columbia University, and became a free-lance writer. His door to the art world was the Newark Museum, where he built up its collection of contemporary American art and pioneered with exhibits of folk art. After eight years at Newark he moved to New

York's Museum of Modern Art, where he was responsible for major shows of folk art and pre-Columbian art.

Cahill's knowledge of American art and artists, his museum and exhibit experience, and his understanding of the victims of the Depression made him a fine choice to head the art project. Even better, he knew that the audience for art had been a limited one, and he wanted to expand it. He believed that art was not only for the wealthy and well educated, but was everyone's birthright, and the masses should be given the opportunity to enjoy it. The Federal Art Project could be the link between art and daily life. Cahill wanted to put the largest possible number of artists to work. From that fermenting mass a few great artists might eventually emerge. But "great" or not, all would help form the connection between art and everyday living.

Cahill set about devising the best possible projects for artists on relief. They must be given not only work, he said, but room for artistic expression and growth. Every director on Federal One (the general name for all the arts projects) had to operate within the limits of bureaucracy and politics. Still, Cahill did his best to encourage a healthy and free atmosphere. Few of the artists who worked on WPA recall any bounds set to their artistic freedom.

Cahill and his five regional directors knew the project stood on quicksand. They were governed by a yearly appropriation whose primary aim was to keep artists fed, clothed, and housed. The art they might produce was a by-product. That the art would prove substantial and valuable seems, in retrospect, to have been a miracle. What it meant to the artist is told by Jacob Kainen. He moved from the relief rolls to the graphic arts division in its first month:

I can testify to the enthusiasm and good will felt by participating artists. Aside from the relief at being able to survive economically, we were grateful to the government for recognizing that art was a public concern. It was good to know that we could function full-time as artists and work in a spirit of camaraderie with other artists and with master craftsmen. We had been given a strong professional motivation at a crucial time, and we appreciated it.

Within a year, over 5,000 artists were busy on the WPA. How were they hired? First, they had to be on relief. Since local relief boards determined eligibility for relief, there was no single standard. What could get you on relief in one town would keep you off it in another. In New York City, where I went on relief, the Home Relief Bureau put applicants through a stiff investigation. Did I have any property—a home, car, oil well, gold mine, shoe store, stocks, bonds? Did anyone in my family have property? Did I have money stashed in my mattress or in a savings account? Did I have insurance that could be cashed in? The relief investigator asked a million questions and took my word for nothing. He checked up on all my answers. Once I was put on the relief rolls, the probing didn't stop. Investigators could drop into my dingy room without notice and look into the icebox or the cupboard to see if I had extra food stored away. The closet was ransacked to see if there was more clothing in it than my relief payment could afford. My neighbors were drawn into the investigation. Did my comings and goings indicate that I might have a secret job? Was I living too high off the hog for a reliefer? Was a brother or a mother in sight who might be able to support me?

I passed safely through this narrow filter and got my

relief check regularly. This, by the way, was an improvement over the previous method of paying out relief. Earlier, food, clothing, and household goods were handed out directly, and rent and utility bills were paid in vouchers. Thus, everyone knew you were on relief. Many people were too proud to accept this humiliating form of handout. The check system eliminated it.

If you made it on relief, there was yet another hurdle to leap. The state WPA project had to accept you. And again, standards varied widely. Was it the quality of the artist's work? Who would judge it? By what criteria? Often it came down to proving you had been a professional. That meant showing you had made money from your art. Young people who had not yet been employed as artists showed their portfolios or a recommendation from their school.

Throughout WPA the law required state administrators to pay the prevailing wage rate in the area for each type of work. The great majority of WPAers outside the arts projects were construction workers. Their pay was about $60 a month. The workers on the arts projects were on a higher wage scale as professionals and also because most were concentrated in urban areas where costs were higher. The man-year allotment for the arts projects averaged $1,200, or about $100 a month. (That difference between $60 and $100 angered many congressmen, who demanded either pay cuts or the complete abolition of the arts projects.)

Cahill soon found that WPA rules devised for masses of construction workers collectively engaged on huge projects did not work well with individual artists. To make artists report daily to timekeepers and sign in for work was silly. By the nature of their work, artists work best at times and in places of their own choosing. An artist caught up in the excitement of a painting often works for eighteen hours without stopping. But the timekeeper said nine-to-five was the schedule. To the petty official any other way of working was "bohemian."

If artists showed the results of their work to a supervisor, said Cahill, wouldn't that be proof enough that they had put in the required hours? Hopkins was willing to try this honor system, but most state administrators refused. The result? Mabel Dwight, an esteemed printmaker living on Staten Island and an older woman handicapped by deafness, feared she would not hear her morning alarm go off. So she sat up nights to make sure she would catch the ferry to Manhattan in time to sign in at the WPA office. If a timekeeper came around to check and she wasn't there, she could be reported as absent without leave. Then she turned around and went all the way back home to work.

The amount each artist had to produce was also subject to rules. Three weeks was the allotted time for a watercolor or gouache, and, depending upon its size, four to six weeks for an oil. Timetables were also set for work by graphic artists, sculptors, and muralists. The larger projects in the cities set up central workshops with cubicles for each painter. There, clocked by the timekeeper, the artist would be sure to put in the required ninety hours a month.

Like any organization, public or private, the project had supervisors. "Their role," said Audrey McMahon, director of the art project in New York,

> was to help the artist secure what was needed and give him comfort and support and then present his work properly to the allocation committee. Supervisors were chosen for their ability to lead people and to guide and help. They were chosen to relate rather than to teach. The only instruction per se was that which a supervising

muralist would give his assistants. But an easel painter or a printmaker was on his own.

The supervisor visited the studios of muralists, but the easel painter or graphic artist brought in his finished work. Works created on the project were allocated to public or semipublic institutions—schools, libraries, hospitals, courthouses, and the like. Muralists, of course, planned their work for a specific place, but many artists never knew where their work went—or if it went anywhere. The work of some artists was not wanted by public officials (which didn't mean they would be dismissed).

Looking back upon it decades later, the art historian Barbara Rose said:

The WPA radically altered the relationship of art and the artist to the art audience and to society. . . . By affording artists the opportunity—which most had never had—to paint full time, the WPA gave them a sense of professionalism previously unattainable outside the academic context. By giving artists materials and time, it allowed them to develop their skills and experience to a new level. Throwing artists together in communal enterprises, the WPA experience provided an *esprit de corps* that carried over into the forties.

8 AN ALMOST INFINITE VARIETY

To the public, the WPA artists gave an almost infinite variety and quality of work and socially useful services. About half of the project workers were engaged in the creative arts. What they contributed, the official record shows, was over 100,000 easel paintings in oil, watercolor, tempera, and pastel; nearly 18,000 pieces of sculpture; about 2,500 murals; and some 250,000 prints of over 11,000 original designs in the graphic media.

By far the largest group of artists on the project was the easel painters. At its peak, there were 900 of them. They included artists of every school or movement: romantic landscape and seascape painters, painters of the social scene, portraitists, academics, abstractionists, expressionists. The landscapes, street scenes, and still lifes done in the romantic manner of the academic style were usually allocated quickly. But no one pressured the artists to paint what was popular. They enjoyed the freedom to express what they wished in the way they chose. Cahill did not believe in dictating subject or style.

Naturally, the artists were influenced by the times they

lived in. The Great Depression turned many Americans to examining the nature of their society. They wanted to know what was wrong and how and why it had come to this crisis. Historians, economists, sociologists were analyzing the available information, and artists were commenting in their own special language. There were many WPA painters who sought to communicate a social message through their work. Among them were Philip Evergood, Robert Gwathmey, Joseph Hirsch, Jacob Lawrence, Jack Levine, Gregorio Prestopino, Walter Quirt, and Philip Reisman. With hundreds of others they formed the American Artists Congress, dedicated to the fight against fascism.

Joseph Solman, who worked in New York's easel division, pointed out what made them so politically conscious:

> The WPA artist quickly became aware of his social environment: first, because he had to go through the gauntlet of home relief before he was eligible to be employed by the Project; second, because he felt an inevitable alliance with the new surge of trade unionism for unskilled workers (CIO) sweeping the country; third, the heated discussions taking place everywhere concerning the New Deal, the welfare state, socialism and communism in the USSR, particularly as depicted by the heroic films of Pudovkin and Eisenstein. The artist became a self-esteemed citizen of his country feeling his product was a viable commodity and beneficial to it.

Useful though they may have felt, artists could never count on continued government support. Jackson Pollock was one of the painters who had his ups and downs on the project's roller coaster. He joined the easel division in

August, 1935, and left it for the last time early in 1943. In between he was fired and rehired several times. In his eight years on the WPA he earned about $7,800—less than $1,000 a year. But he said, long after, "I'm grateful to the WPA for keeping me alive during the Thirties." Those years permitted him to live freely, developing the personal style that was to earn him international renown as an abstractionist. When the WPA ended, he was obliged for a time to earn his living by decorating ties and lipsticks.

Trying to describe the difference between the two major styles of the thirties—regionalism and social realism— Richard D. McKinzie said of them:

> The major differences in the two views lay in the degree of nativism each embraced and the amount of social comment each thought appropriate. When a regionalist painted a farmer plowing under his crop, the social realist charged, somewhat unfairly, that the viewer could not tell whether the artist condoned or condemned [the act]. . . . Like the regionalist, the social realist's art was impersonal and his forms and figures were clearly recognizable, but it focused more on the abstractions of politics and social justice. More strongly than the re-gionalist, the social realist commented on what he ob-served, intent on involving the viewer in the issue. . . . These visual editorials of the contemporary scene had a more immediate than lasting appeal. By the end of the 1930's, when some of the earlier work lost its relevance, other ideas began to eclipse contemporary realism.

Expressionists were considered aesthetically subversive at the time, says Joseph Solman, who was one of them. (Other expressionists on the project included Mark Rothko, Herman Rose, Jack Tworkov, and Alice Neel.) "The art climate," he said, "was predominately Woodstock (Alexander Brook), social protest (Shahn and Mexican influence), and American Western (Benton, Curry and Wood). We were outcasts on the scene; only John Marin and Max Weber, and to a smaller extent Stuart Davis, Hartley, Knaths and Avery were tolerated as representatives of the growing modern tradition."

The Mexican influence Solman refers to had a direct effect upon many of the WPA artists. Leading Mexican muralists—Diego Rivera, José Clemente Orozco, David Alfaro Siqueiros—were working in the United States and hiring young American assistants. Jackson Pollock and Axel Horn, who had become friends in Benton's class and were now both on the WPA, joined a workshop on West Fourteenth Street that Siqueiros opened to experiment with new tools and new materials. Horn recalled that experience and its impact:

> Paints including the then new nitro-cellulose lacquers and silicones, surfaces such as plywood and asbestos panels and paint applicators including airbrushes and spray-guns were some of the materials and techniques to be explored and applied. We were going to put out to pasture the "stick with hairs on its end" as Siqueiros called the brush.
>
> New art forms for . . . exposure to large masses of people were to be initiated. Our stated aim was to perfect such new media even though they might be comparatively impermanent, since they would be seen by hundreds of thousands of people in the form of floats, posters, changeable murals in subways multi-reproduced graphics, etc.
>
> Spurred on by Siqueiros, whose energy and torrential flow of ideas and new projects stimulated us all to a high

pitch of activity, everything became material for our investigations. For instance: lacquer opened up enormous possibilities for application of color. We sprayed through stencils and friskets, embedded wood, metal, sand and paper. We used it in thin glazes or built it up into thick gobs. We poured it, dripped it, spattered it, hurled it at the picture surface. It dried quickly, almost instantly, and could be removed at will even though thoroughly dry and hard. What emerged was an endless variety of accidental effects. . . .

Of course, we used all these devices to enhance paintings with literary content. No one thought of them as ends in themselves. The genesis of Pollock's mature art began to be discernible only when he began to exploit these techniques as final statement.

It should be noted here that the technical divisions of the Federal Art Project deserve credit for new materials and methods. Their ingenuity produced two synthetic resins, alkyd and acrylic; a noncrackable sizing for canvas; a technique for painting directly on plastered walls by mixing a special glue with paint; and the petrochrome mural.

Some of the new methods and materials came into play when the Artists Union created a Public Use of Art Committee. Said Horn:

We wanted to promote the fact that the Federal Art Project served the people and should be supported for that reason, not just because it fed hungry artists. The great concern of Siqueiros and the other Mexican muralists for art as a social force stirred us to try to create a new artistic language. We went to great lengths to strengthen the artists' sense of community and responsibility to it.

As the thirties wore on, many artists lost interest in illustrating American life. Matisse and Picasso seemed more vital to them than the realists. The French modernists led Americans to experiment with nonrepresentational art. There were only a small number of abstract artists around New York in the early thirties. When the WPA came along, it provided the fertile environment for them to create—free "from the pressure of clique, the insistence of dealers, the noise of publicity," as Constance Rourke put it. Their work was rarely rejected by the WPA, even though it was abstract. A member of this group, Rosalind Bengelsdorf Browne, speaks of the abstract artists as a "truly dedicated minority, determined to win acceptance and understanding. We organized the American Abstract Artists, we exhibited, and we proselytized via our most articulate spokesmen and skilled writers." But it was the Federal Art Project, she stresses, that "created our immediate and most valuable audience—an audience of our peers. It is entirely conceivable that figurative artists of the 1930's, who are internationally famous for an abstract idiom today, were stirred to experiment partly by our arduous efforts to spread abstract gospel then."

Despite their excitement and zeal, abstract artists were attacked as though they were some sort of disease bent on infecting the healthy native American art. Abstract art was damned as art for art's sake, while realism was extolled as the genuine American expression. Several of the abstractionists answered the assault through a letter appearing in a 1937 issue of *Art Front*, the magazine of the Artists Union. It read, in part:

We abstract artists are, of course, first to recognize that any good work of art has its own justification, that it has the effect of bringing joyful ecstasy to a sensitive spectator, that there is such a thing as an esthetic emotion, which is a particular emotion, caused by a particular created harmony of lines, colors and forms. . . .

It is our very definite belief that abstract art forms are not separated from life, but on the contrary are great realities, manifestations of a search into the world about one's self, having basis in living actuality, made by artists who walk the earth, who see colors (which are realities), squares (which are realities, not some spiritual mystery), tactile surfaces, resistant materials, movement. The abstract work of an artist who is not conscious of it or is contemptuous of the world about him is different from the abstract work of an artist who identifies himself with life and seeks generative force from its realities. . . .

Abstract art does not end in a private chapel. Its positive identification with life has brought a profound change in our environment and in our lives. The modern esthetic has accompanied modern science in a quest for knowledge and recognition of materials in a search for a logical combination of art and life. In no other age has art functioned so ubiquitously as in our own. One has only to observe the life about him to see that abstract art has been enormously fecund, and remains a vitally organic reality of this age.

The widest range of the various styles of the thirties is seen in the murals painted by the artists on the Federal Art Project. It was usually not federal buildings that were decorated by WPA murals. These were the preserve of the two art sections under the Treasury Department. The WPA confined itself largely to public buildings under state or

local control. Not since the frescoes of the Italian Renaissance and the more recent flowering of the Mexican mural
had the social uses of art for public buildings been so
dramatically expressed. Although these two influences
were dominant in WPA murals, the styles of French acade-
micians and abstractionists, of Oriental decorators, and of
commercial illustrators were visible, too.

Again, this rich variety is attributable to Holger Cahill's
policy of not interfering in style or in source of inspiration.
He saw the Depression as a period of search rather than
synthesis. He once said that "American art is anything
that an American artist does." He meant to discourage
only inferior art, not unorthodox techniques. As for the
charge of propaganda leveled at some of the WPA murals,
Cahill replied that the mural art of great periods always
expressed "social meaning, the experience, history, ideas
and beliefs of a community."

Of course, by the public nature of their work, the
muralists didn't have the same freedom as the easel painter.
The mural had to be acceptable to the sponsors who paid
for all the nonlabor costs. But with careful, diplomatic
planning, few large murals were rejected, even though
modifications were occasionally requested by the sponsors.
The supervisor of mural paintings, together with his scouts,
had to find building, space, and sponsor. It was not easy
to convince a sponsor that wall decoration was desirable,
and that he should pay for materials, scaffolding, and other
incidentals. Once he had agreed, a plan to suit the space
was developed, then an artist who painted in the style for
which the purpose of the building called had to be selected,
and a suitable subject agreed upon. Research on the subject
followed, preliminary sketches were submitted for approval,
a group of assistant artists mustered, and working-site facilities arranged. Innumerable conferences took place all

along the way to ensure the cooperation and consent of the many parties involved in such a communal endeavor.

One of the WPA's best-known muralists was Edward Laning. In the fall of 1935 he was asked to paint the walls of the dining room on Ellis Island, the federal reception center for immigrants to the United States. On one 100-foot wall he decided to depict the role of the immigrant in the development of America. It meant research into how steel was made, railroads built, sawmills operated, and coal mined. It was the spring of 1937 before the completed mural was unveiled.

That same year he began a mural for the huge Main Reading Room of the New York Public Library. The theme was the story of the recorded word: Moses and the tablets of the Law, the medieval scribe and his manuscript, Gutenberg and the first printing press, and Mergenthaler with his linotype machine. Early in 1942 the four mural panels and two lunettes were finished and installed.

Thirty years later, Laning said the Federal Art Project "was my life as artist and mural painter." He knew now, he went on, that the thirties was "our Golden Age, the only humane era in our history, the one brief period when we permitted ourselves to be good. Before that time, all was Business, and after, it all has been War."

In the early stages of the project, mural work and art teaching were given the greatest attention. Easel painting was considered a precious field only for the few. Such distinguished painters as Herman Rose had to spend months away from their easels, assisting the muralists. Some of the best modernists, however, got a chance to try their art on walls. Karl Knaths, Stuart Davis, Arshile Gorky, Louis Schanker, and Willem de Kooning became the first to develop the abstract style in American mural painting.

De Kooning, born in the Netherlands, had entered the United States illegally in 1926. Only twenty-two, he thought he could make money easily in America, the golden land. He would get rich quick, then have all the time he wanted to paint. But like most young artists, he had to support himself with odd jobs: house painting, carpentry, making signs, assembling department-store displays. As soon as the Federal Art Project started, he said:

> I got on the WPA, and I met all kinds of other painters and sculptors and writers and poets and architects, all in the same boat, because America never really cared much for people who do those things. I was on the Project about a year or a year and a half, and that really made it stick, this attitude, because the amount of money we made on the Project was rather fair; in the Depression days one could live modestly and nicely. So I felt, well, I have to just keep doing that. The decision to take was: was it worth it to put all my eggs in one basket, that kind of basket of art?

The answer came out of his work. On the WPA, de Kooning was given several mural projects. Although none was ever finally commissioned, his study for a big housing project mural was exhibited at the Museum of Modern Art in New York in 1936 in a showing of works by project artists. It was his first public appearance. Later, he said, "I had to resign because I was an alien, but even the year I was on gave me such a terrific feeling that I gave up painting on the side and took a different attitude. After the Project I decided to paint and do odd jobs on the side. The situation was the same, but I had a different attitude."

The Soyer brothers, Raphael and Moses, Russian-born

artists who became outstanding American painters, both worked on the art project in New York City. David Soyer, the son of Moses, recalls those days:

> Moses' studio was in an ancient building off Columbus Circle that had once housed a medical school. The wide stone stairs had deep grooves in them from years of use, and the halls still smelled of formaldehyde and ether. . . . The official WPA business of this studio was murals for public buildings. One was of children playing, to be placed in the children's ward of a Brooklyn hospital. Another was a panoramic view of Philadelphia for a post office in that city. Months after the Philadelphia mural had been completed and installed, a priest noticed that the cross atop his church was missing from the painting. A hurry-up trip to the City of Brotherly Love, paint box in hand, and the desecration was repaired. It may have been flattering that in a busy post office someone had looked closely enough at the mural to notice such a detail. . . .
>
> Many of Moses' friends and colleagues were called social realists, and some classified Moses with this group. But in his paintings . . . there was just the "message of people" and since it was the depression, this was a message of people in the depression, darkly painted and somber, a heavy-breasted Black woman leaning out of a tenement window, a seamstress, tired dancers, men of the waterfront. There was no need to search for themes or subjects. They were constantly around for there were always people at hand. . . .

The press was overwhelmingly opposed to the New Deal. In murals that expressed social protest, it found a way to attack Roosevelt. It called the murals "un-American,"

A section of the Federal Art Project mural, "The Cycle of a Woman's Life," by Lucienne Bloch. *WPA Photographs, Archives of American Art, Smithsonian Institution*

A master muralist on the WPA working with his assistants. *WPA Photo No. 69-ANA-9E-1 in the National Archives*

Part of a WPA mural painted by Symeon Shimin for the Justice Department building in Washington, D.C. *Public Buildings Service Photo No. 121-PS-5629 in the National Archives*

In "The Relief Blues," *WPA* artist Louis O. Guglieme shows the welfare investigator questioning a family on its qualifications for relief—a scene millions of Americans grew familiar with in the thirties. *Courtesy of National Collection of Fine Arts, Smithsonian Institution*

Knaths, Karl. *Composition.* (c. 1937). Gouache, 15¾″ x 22¾″ *On extended loan from the United States WPA Art Program to the Museum of Modern Art, New York* (Top)

The range of media and subjects chosen by sculptors of the Federal Art Project was enormous. "Worker and Child" is by Robert Cronbach. *WPA–FAP Archives of American Art, Smithsonian Institution* (Right)

WPA artist Concetta Scaravaglione working on the plaster model of "Girl with Faun." *WPA–FAP Archives of American Art, Smithsonian Institution*

Raphael Soyer's dry point etching of "Cafeteria." *Courtesy of National Collection of Fine Arts, Smithsonian Institution*

"Labor," by Will Barnet. *Courtesy of National Collection of Fine Arts, Smithsonian Institution*

"communistic," "tripe," "junk," "disgusting." In Chicago, after such a barrage, the school board plastered over a mural on "Women's Contribution to American Progress." There were many cases of attempted censorship. But such interference was outweighed by the satisfaction of most sponsors and the many awards won by the artists. Because the WPA murals were what most people saw, they soon became associated with "government art."

Compared with the number of painters on the project, sculptors were relatively few. At its peak, there were about 500, and nearly half worked in New York City. California had about 75, and Chicago, 50. The rest were scattered in about twenty other states. Sculpture in the thirties was basically of two kinds—one, made to exhibit in a gallery (called "pedestal" sculpture), and the other conceived for a particular environment (called "monumental" or "architectural" sculpture).

Sculpture technique had not changed much for many years. Most sculptors worked in clay and then cast in bronze, cast stone, or terra-cotta. But some had begun to carve directly in wood or stone, and a small number were pioneering with the welding torch and industrial tools in the direct working of metal.

While the WPA provided central workshops and storage space, most sculptors worked in their own studios on materials supplied by the project. Regulations required them to give fifteen hours a week to sculpture, which later became the project's property. Many, of course, put in far more time, forty to sixty hours. Supervisors visited their studios to check on the work. Hired hands? No one felt that way. On the contrary, here they were, at a time when the private market for art was almost zero, drawing a weekly wage to work in their own studios as artists. A WPA sculptor, Robert Cronbach, said:

It was an unequalled opportunity for a serious artist to work as steadily and intensely as possible to advance the quality of his art. . . . There is something inherently sound and stimulating about the fact of a large number of artists working steadily at a flat wage which is neither disastrously low nor high enough to be of great importance. This puts the emphasis where it should be, on esthetic questions, esthetic competition, one's relationship to and status among one's peers, not on winning prize money or a popularity contest.

The pedestal sculptor received no instructions from the project. What he created became part of an extensive exhibition program. His work might be seen in many of the major museums and galleries. And like the easel paintings, sculpture was loaned or given permanently to schools, libraries, public offices, courthouses, and hospitals.

When the opportunity came to plan sculpture for a particular public site, the supervisors discussed it with the artists. Anyone who was interested would work out a study and scale model. When the model was approved by the sponsor, the sculptor went to work. Sculptors were free to participate or not in such architectural projects. If they chose to, and their models were rejected, they simply went on with their pedestal work. They were under no economic pressure because they continued to draw their regular weekly pay. They could thus afford to do whatever they wanted, to be as experimental and venturesome as they liked. The only stake was recognition and status among their fellow artists. It was, said Cronbach, "a stimulating environment of excitement and challenge, and of comradeship."

The figurative sculptors were the largest group on the project. Many were strongly influenced by the climate of social consciousness. A number of them based their work on the human image, influenced by the abstract sculptural qualities of such artists as Alexander Archipenko, Henry Moore, Ossip Zadkine, and Jacques Lipchitz. This kind of sculpture, exemplified in the work of Milton Hebald and Cronbach, became identified as the closest thing to a project style. A few other sculptors experimented with other styles—abstractionism, constructivism, or surrealism. Welded metal sculpture, begun in Europe, was developed here by the WPA artist David Smith. There was a continual circulation of ideas and techniques among the project sculptors. The meetings organized by the Artists Union served as forums for that exchange. At one of them, for instance, David Smith demonstrated his welding methods. Eventually out of his work there developed a New York school that included such famous sculptors as Herbert Ferber, David Hare, Seymour Lipton, José de Rivera, and Theodore Roszak.

9 ART FOR THE PEOPLE

Early in February, 1936, a studio workshop for graphic artists opened in the Federal Art Project headquarters in New York. In it were special presses for printing etchings, lithographs, and woodcuts; several kinds of tables to work on; and a tank and wooden grill for graining lithography stones. Graphic artists could select the kind of lithography stone they wanted, the papers, woods, copperplates—whatever tools and materials they needed for the various techniques of printmaking. Six months after the WPA's graphic division was formed, artists could come to see demonstrations of the processes of etching, lithography, and block printing.

Such printing workshops set up by the WPA prepared the ground for the flowering of the graphic arts in the United States. When the graphic division was established, printmaking had long labored under a stuffy tradition that limited both what artists could express and the media they could use. Most of the graphic artists were engravers, using only copperplates. Lithographers and wood engravers were in the minority. The nonconformists were ignored by both collectors and professional print societies.

It was project leaders like Audrey McMahon of New York who saw what printmaking could do to unite the artist with the people. By the very nature of the medium, the print could be a democratic influence. Prints were portable and they were cheap. Allocated to schools, libraries, museums, hospitals, government offices, and army bases, they could broaden public understanding and appreciation of the creative arts.

The New York project took on some 85 printmakers. Other states followed until about 250 artists were at work nationally. Most of the prints came out of a few centers: New York, Chicago, Cleveland, Philadelphia, and San Francisco.

The printmakers, like other WPA artists, were at first subjected to the idiocy of the timekeeper, but regulations were soon made more sensible. Artists submitted sketches to a supervisor. Upon approval, they received a block or plate, or stone, and took it home to work. If they preferred, they could do the lithograph, engraving, or woodcut in the workshop. When the time came for proofing their block, plate, or stone, they worked in the shop on the printing. When the proofs were satisfactory, the entire run was printed, from twenty-five to seventy-five prints, but commonly twenty-five. (The artist was allowed to keep three prints for himself.) The production quota was one graphic work a month.

Working at the central shop had some disadvantages. It meant extra carfare, the expense of meals out, and keeping to restricted hours. Also, the artist was under the constant eye of fellow artists, who watched as he tried to make crucial decisions. But this sometimes brought unexpected

rewards. Jacob Kainen tells of a day when he—a novice—
was drawing on a stone in the shop and the eminent Stuart
Davis came by:

> Inspired by his presence I made some bold decisions,
> almost reckless ones, that gave some verve and sparkle
> to the composition. It was probably the best print I
> made on the Project. I still remember with pleasure his
> kind words: "That's damn good." If more artists of
> Davis' caliber could have given us some personal atten-
> tion, even if only to watch us at work, I am sure we
> would have taken some unaccustomed chances and
> moved ahead in our art.

Despite the difficulties of a WPA relief project, most
printmakers felt at home in their workshop. The supervisors took no sides on aesthetic issues, but they encouraged
technical exploration. The younger printmakers, especially,
were stimulated by working alongside such distinguished
artists as Davis, Adolph Dehn, Yasuo Kuniyoshi, and
Raphael Soyer. The subjects most frequently chosen by
the printmakers reflected the crisis they shared with all
Americans. But the strongest among them responded in
individual ways to the modern directions in art—abstrac-
tion, surrealism, and expressionism.

Several new techniques came out of the graphic arts
division. In Philadelphia the black artist Dox Thrash and
four co-workers developed a new carborundum printing
process and the carborundum etching color process. In
New York, improvements were made in color lithography
and block printing. It was a group under the direction of
Anthony Velonis that developed the silk-screen process
into a fine arts medium. Color prints, not then mass-
produced, earned a wide popularity. The color woodcut,

developed in the WPA graphic division under Louis Schanker's guidance, won support from American artists.

Within a year of the first experiments, a fifth of the project's prints were being reproduced by the silk-screen process. This versatile method permitted printing on glass, wood, cloth, and almost any solid substance. It could be used for commercial mass production or to reproduce masterpieces, as the Museum of Modern Art soon demonstrated with works from its own collection. Critics praised the work, and museums exhibited the prints.

The WPA's poster group made a ready adaptation of their art to public service. The messages of federal, state, and municipal agencies were spread everywhere by ingenious and aesthetic posters printed by graphic artists. By mid-1940, some 500 poster artists had provided 1.6 million posters from 30,500 original designs. These posters promoted fire prevention, prenatal care, noise abatement, better housing, the reading of books, treatment of venereal disease, good nutrition, consumer interests, and a thousand other good causes. So cheap and effective was this product, that these artists could count on support from nearly every government agency.

Like the poster artists, the photographers on the project served both the WPA itself and other units of government. They photographed everything from construction projects to material for publicity handouts. They also photographed a great many works produced on the art project, thus preserving a record of them for the Archives of American Art. They learned to make photo murals and photo posters. One of their finest artists, Berenice Abbott, documented New York life. A selection of her photographs were published in the book *Changing New York*. Altogether the WPA produced almost 500,000 photographs and over 15,000 slides.

While experiments with techniques were welcomed by the project administration, Jacob Kainen, discussing it recently, feels that more could have been done to encourage aesthetic exploration. He believes it was "no accident" that the big change in American art came shortly after the project ended. The consistent years of work on the WPA made possible such "rapid" and "far-reaching" development:

The printmaking workshops that were set up in the 1930s were pioneer centers for technical and artistic growth, and the artists who worked there formed a solid basis for further development. They popularized lithography, the woodcut, serigraphy, and most of all color printing. When the projects ended they joined the staffs of schools and universities which increasingly added printmaking departments. These artists knew how to set up workshops and they knew all the media. And so, for the first time in the history of American graphic arts, students found a large number of instructors who practised and welcomed fresh approaches. When Stanley William Hayter came to this country in 1940 to open his experimental graphic arts studio, Atelier 17, he found the artists ready.

Happily for the country, Holger Cahill was just as interested in American folk art and crafts as in contemporary works. In his first museum posts he renewed the interest in American art and craftsmanship that had had wide popularity in the late nineteenth century. He collected examples of early American paintings (the "primitives"), Indian artifacts, Shaker furniture, and Spanish Colonial objects—all of which were reminders that there was a tradition of an American people's art.

In 1933, in his introduction to the Folk Art Exhibition at the Museum of Modern Art, Cahill reviewed the achievements of America's early anonymous artists who had worked in various mediums, and underscored their significance as an expression of our national experience. The Federal Art Project offered a much broader opportunity to create, as he said, "a great reservoir of art in many forms as a vital function of society." By establishing the Index of American Design, Cahill and the WPA rescued from oblivion the creations of innumerable talented Americans.

Credit for the idea of the Index belongs to Ruth Reeves, a textile designer and printer, and to Romana Javitz, head of the New York Public Library's Picture Collection. They discussed the need to make a documentary pictorial record of the useful and popular arts of the American people. Such invaluable records of native design were to be found in Europe, Mexico, China, and Japan, but there had never been one prepared for America. Out of her rich experience, Miss Javitz drafted a proposal for Miss Reeves to submit to the newly formed Federal Art Project in 1935.

Cahill's response was warm but cautious. To attempt a pictorial record of design in the American decorative, folk, and practical arts from their inception to about 1890 seemed a fantastic undertaking; he guessed it would require at least twenty years to accomplish. And who knew whether the WPA would endure for even six months? But if the Index could be done at all, it would need a federal agency to do it. It could muster the finances and could employ hundreds of artists to compile the enormous pictorial and documentary record. Looking beyond, training them in this work would maintain and improve their professional competence for careers in commercial art. More designers and more manufacturers, Cahill argued, could use the Index not as something to initiate "but as pollen—or what you please—with which to fertilize contemporary design."

Early in 1936, the plan for a nationwide effort was ready. Miss Reeves was the first chief of the Index, followed by C. Adolph Glassgold, and then Benjamin Knotts. Constance Rourke, an authority on American craftsmanship and culture, was national editor. Besides its relief functions, the Index had three aims:

1. To record material of historical significance that hadn't been studied before and that stood in danger of being lost.

2. To gather a body of traditional material that could form the basis of an organic development of American design.

3. To make usable source records of this material accessible to artists, designers, manufacturers, museums, libraries, and art schools.

At its peak, the Index was staffed by about 500 workers in 35 states. More could easily have been employed, but Cahill insisted on a high level of competence. In the six years of its life, the Index made 22,000 plates (about a third of them photographic studies).

Research teams went to work in all corners of America, seeking out examples of American design and craftsmanship in ceramics, costumery, glass, furniture, metalworking, textiles, and wood carving. (Indian design was left to the ethnologists, and architecture to two other New Deal projects.) Regional and local crafts were stressed. Examples were crewelwork, the Shaker crafts of New England and New York State, the German crafts of Colonial Pennsylvania, the pioneer furniture and tools of the Midwest, the ironwork of Maryland and Louisiana, and the weaving and wood carving of the Spanish of the Southwest. Included, too, were carousel horses, cigar-store Indians, quilts, tavern signs, figureheads, pots and pans, and painting as home art and as the work of sign painters and decorators.

The staff was trained to use a meticulous technique of documentary painting in watercolor that was developed on an Egyptian expedition by Joseph Lindon Smith. But soon other precision methods for recording design were devised—some using oils. If color was not important, pen and pencil were used. And photography, of course, proved best for many items. Whatever the method, the supervisors insisted on scholarly, artistic work that "must equal or exceed in quality the finest publications in design ever produced."

In the beginning, the artists looked down upon their assignment as "dead copying." But the freedom to devise new techniques, the achievement of high quality in the plates, and the enthusiasm of the art journals for the Index restored their pride. Cahill wrote:

What was insisted upon was strict objectivity, accurate drawing, clarity of construction, exact proportions, and faithful rendering of material, color and texture so that each Index drawing might stand as surrogate for the object. . . . The best drawings, while maintaining complete fidelity to the object, have the individuality which characterizes works of art. To find their peers in American art one must go back to the still-life of William Harnett and the trompe-l'oeil painters of the nineteenth century.

Cahill hoped the completed Index would be on the shelves of every library, school, and museum in the country. He saw it as a standard reference tool for artists and craftsmen, designers, manufacturers, historians, educators, and students. To make it accurate meant publication in full-color reproduction. Neither government, nor commercial publishers, nor nonprofit associations were willing to undertake such a huge and costly task. As the country moved into World War II, the project was closed down before its work was finished. Eventually the National Gallery of Art in the Smithsonian Institution at Washington took the collection of completed plates and opened a room where artists and designers could use them. Circulating exhibitions and slide lectures brought the plates before much wider audiences. Many of the plates have now been published in two books, Erwin O. Christensen's *The Index of American Design* (with 400 plates) and Clarence P. Hornung's *Treasury of American Design* (with 900 plates).

The Index of American Design did more than record the design of the past. It popularized American folk art, breaking through the small circle of connoisseurs to reach the nation. In Constance Rourke's words, it offered "an education of the eye, particularly for young people, which may result in the development of taste and a genuine consciousness of our rich national inheritance."

But the Index, great though its achievement was, was only an incidental instrument of mass education. To the artistically illiterate layman, the community art centers developed by the project were its most valuable activity. Until the WPA, art education for nonprofessionals was pathetically limited. In very few places in this huge land could the layman learn anything about art. The settlement houses tried, and so did some of the art museums, but the teachers were often untrained and the courses were more crafts than fine arts. Only the small number of children's museums did better. It took the Depression and the Federal Art Project to launch a significant art-center movement.

As early as 1935 Daniel Defenbacher of the North Carolina project established three centers in his state. Each had galleries for exhibits, and each offered classes for adults and children, gallery talks, and demonstrations of various art techniques and mediums. Within a year there were twenty-five WPA art centers in the South and West, and a million people, young and old, had taken part in their programs. By 1941 there were over a hundred art centers, with WPA labor putting up new buildings to house some of them. They gave frequent shows of local, regional, and national art; they offered free lectures, films, classes, workshops, cultural events, and meeting rooms for community activities. Art, up until then a stranger to thousands of communities, was becoming an experience to be shared by all who came to the WPA centers. Staff, exhibits, and some of the equipment were supplied by the WPA. Community sponsors donated the buildings or paid the cost of rent and utilities while they helped to shape the program.

The proportion of project workers engaged in art education never rose above 25 percent. By far the larger number was engaged in creating art. Nevertheless, an impressive start was made in educating the masses, for whom art also presumably exists. The centers offered recreational art classes for everyone who wanted competent guidance. Following progressive principles of education, the greatest freedom for individual expression was offered. Instructors were not out to give grades or impose class standards. They kept their criticism to the individual's own needs, encouraging a competence related to each student's age and experience. The teachers themselves were trained in seminars and refresher courses and supervised through field visits from the national office. There were "open" classes for the amateur who wanted only leisure-time pleasure, and more rigorous "guild" classes for those who came with a certain level of skill. By 1941, WPA art courses covered twenty-three subjects, from ceramics to photography.

The children's classes were the core of the WPA program. Thousands were reached not only in the art centers but in settlement houses, service clubs, orphanages, day nurseries, churches, hospitals—wherever the young were to be found. Some centers held children's classes daily. In New York City 50,000 children and adults were reached weekly by WPA teachers. In Washington, D.C., the Children's Gallery reached 3,000 a month, and in addition offered classes and provided exhibits in public schools and other places.

Harlem provides one of the best examples of what the WPA community art centers did. For black people, poverty had been chronic ever since Emancipation. The great migration North during and after World War I had made Harlem the largest black community in the world. Like other ghettos it had its slums, but it had its artists, too—men and women who were beginning to give a voice to black America. The young artists and writers created the Black Renaissance of the twenties. In their work they protested against injustice and inequality, they explored the black past—a history neglected and distorted by white scholars—and they discovered the richness of their African background and the variety of their folk culture.

When the stock market crashed, a life that had never been bountiful became even worse. Proportionately more blacks than whites lost their jobs. Their immediate problem was survival. Black artists formed the Harlem Artists Guild to fight for jobs and fair treatment on the WPA. In 1935, when the Federal Art Project was formed, there were almost no blacks among the New York City workers. But two years later there were over a hundred, including supervisors. Art historian Milton W. Brown describes what the drive of black artists for recognition and sustenance accomplished:

There was no color line on the art projects, and for the first time Black artists, as well as white, were given the opportunity to practice their art full-time. They became equal members of a community fighting for what they believed to be the rights of all artists in a civilized society. This interplay, and it occurred in all the arts, had a telling effect on racial relations in the United States. Those artists who were on the projects were formed by the experience.

The Harlem Art Center at One Hundred Twenty-fifth Street and Lenox Avenue had a central gallery flanked by studios equipped for study and work. Within a year, the center was serving over 3,000 students. Besides holding many exhibitions, the center became a meeting place for community and project organizations. But its heart was its classes. Artists such as Charles Alston, Henry Bannarn, Gwendolyn Bennett, and Augusta Savage worked there as supervisors and teachers. They helped raise a younger generation of black artists, among them Romare Bearden, Jacob Lawrence, Ernest Crichlow, and Norman Lewis. But the center's reputation was so good it attracted many of the city's most talented young artists, regardless of color. All wanted to enjoy the advantages of a training that was equal to the best the city's professional art schools could offer.

What happened to Jacob Lawrence is an example of the impact of the Harlem Art Center. As a youngster, he started to learn about art in an after-school program at a Harlem settlement called Utopia House. Charles Alston, then a young recreational director, recognized Lawrence's

unique talent, and encouraged him. Soon Lawrence moved
on to the Harlem Art Workshop set up by the WPA,
going to high school at the same time and doing all sorts
of odd jobs to keep eating. At seventeen he spent six
months working in a CCC camp in upstate New York. He
returned to the city to paint his first Harlem scenes at the
Harlem Art Center. But there was less and less time to
paint as he scurried around trying to earn money. That
necessity came terribly close to forcing him out of art. In
their portrait of Lawrence, Romare Bearden and Harry
Henderson tell the story:

> He gradually came to think of painting as something
> he would do as a hobby. And he was beginning to see
> that without an education, he was going to be per-
> manently lined up for menial jobs. As one job played
> out, he found another. But one day, when he dropped
> into the Harlem Art Center, Augusta Savage said, "Come
> on, Jake. We're going to the WPA. . . . You're old
> enough now. . . ."
>   It was July 1938 and he was now 21. He was ac-
> cepted as an artist and assigned to the easel project. He
> could paint at home and was provided with materials
> and $23.86 a week. In return he had to deliver two
> paintings every six weeks.
>   Later, looking back, Jake said, "If Augusta Savage
> hadn't insisted on getting me on the project, I would
> never have become an artist. It was a real turning point
> for me."
>   During the 18 months he was on the WPA project
> Jake had time to develop his technique in working with
> water-based paints, which he preferred to oils. More
> importantly, it established him as an artist in his own
> mind and gave him confidence in the value of his work.

And when he picked up his pay check at WPA headquarters, he met many other artists and writers, both
Black and white. This gave him a broader perspective
on all the arts. It also deepened his own interest in the
area he knew best: the lives of Black people and their
history.

The editor of *Art News*, Thomas B. Hess, sees the thirties in a special light. The history books recall the Depression years as a bleak, sad time. Hess agrees that for older
people especially "it was harsh indeed: they had lost their
money, their sense of being able to cope with life, their
belief in themselves and in the future. It was equally
painful for children who watched their parents mourn for
lost businesses, worry about the next month's rent, talk
endlessly about money."

But for young artists? It was different, Hess claims, and
he tells why:

> . . . for the young men and women of the decade, espe-
> cially the artists, writers, and their friends, it was a
> tremendously gay period. The whole question of money
> suddenly disappeared and everybody could do as he
> pleased. David Smith told me that parties were never
> as wonderful as in the 1930s, when everyone chipped
> in for whiskey and all the girls were beautiful. . . .
> Harold Rosenberg remembers demonstration parades for
> the workers; contingents of artists carried cardboard
> palettes, writers brandished big cardboard pens, one
> young writer carried a sign proclaiming, "WE WANT BON-
> VIVANT JOBS!"
>
> . . . It was one of those rare moments in history when
> nothing interfered with the discussion [of art]; there
> were no sales, exhibitions, careers. The Impressionists,

in the Cafe Guerbois days, when they were all unknown or despised, must have had a similar moment. Some artists changed styles easily from year to year; others carefully studied the latest issues of *Cahiers d'Art*. A sense of colleaguality and mutual respect marked the community; ideas could be debated seriously with respect for different opinions.

The artists at first may have huddled together in Greenwich Village out of a sense of mutual protection, but they stayed together because they found that they could become their own audience. They lived in lofts, had their favorite park benches in the spring and cafeteria tables in the winter. They belonged. It was out of this lively community that came the great flowering of postwar American art.

10 MUSIC IN THE AIR

At the age of fifteen, Richard Kapuscinski took his first step into the world of professional music. He got a summer job on the Federal Music Project in Milwaukee, copying music scores in India ink. The minimum age for hiring on the WPA was twenty-one, but special dispensation was given young Richard because his father, a laborer, was both jobless and too ill to work. The son, studying the cello (on an instrument his brother had found), proved he could copy scores accurately. Later Kapuscinski would play first cello in the Boston Symphony for many years and become head of the chamber music department at Oberlin College.

Music copying was but one of dozens of services the Federal Music Project performed. Begun as a necessary function for the WPA orchestras and music units long before Xerox copying was invented, it soon expanded to service university and public libraries. The Milwaukee unit alone provided more than 2,000 scores for orchestras, bands, choruses, and chamber groups.

American musicians were in a bad way even before the

crash. Unemployment had become chronic. Recordings and then the radio had reduced the demand for "live" music. When the sound film appeared in 1928, over 20,000 musicians lost their jobs in theater orchestras. The Depression swept thousands more out of work. Opera companies canceled seasons, hotels and restaurants eliminated orchestras, music pupils dropped their lessons, and school boards slashed budgets for music and the other arts.

In 1932, when the Roxy Theatre opened in New York, over 3,000 musicians competed for the 80 posts in the pit orchestra. By 1933, two-thirds of the national membership of the American Federation of Musicians was unemployed. In New York City alone, 12,000 of the 15,000 members could find no work. So desperate were the musicians that their union levied a tax of 1 percent on the weekly wages of all its members lucky enough to be working. The money went for the relief of their fellow unionists. Then the union adopted a stagger system. Musicians with regular jobs had to give one week's work in four, or one day's work in seven, to unemployed members.

Private philanthropy also made efforts to provide work relief for musicians. But no matter how generous, they could never meet the need. The early New Deal agencies made a small beginning with public funds. But not until the WPA's Federal One program began in 1935 did this moribund profession get more than superficial aid.

To head the Federal Music Project, Washington chose Nikolai Sokoloff. He was born in Russia where he played the violin with the Kiev Orchestra, conducted by his father. Later he moved to the United States, studied at the Yale School of Music, and eventually became director of the Cleveland Orchestra. When he took the WPA post, at the age of forty-nine, he had been with the Cleveland Orchestra for fifteen years. His prestige ensured the

cooperation of professional musicians in the development
of the project's program.

Insisting upon the highest level of artistic performance,
Sokoloff worked through regional and state directors to
build a concert branch and a music education branch. If
they passed auditions, musicians on relief found work on
the project. Local audition boards screened applicants for
competence in performance. Musicians were desired for all
kinds of performances. The variety can be seen in the
concert division, which in 1939 employed nearly 8,000
musicians. They worked in 28 symphony orchestras, 90
smaller orchestras, 68 bands, 55 dance bands, 15 chamber
music groups, 33 opera and choral units, and a soloists'
unit.

In the larger cities, of course, there were more and
better musicians. The smaller communities had the problem of recruiting enough capable musicians to play the
variety of instruments required for ensembles. In one
Midwestern town, for example, a project supervisor reported he had been able to muster only one violin, one
piano, one bass, one guitar, one saxophone, one accordion,
one clarinet, one drum—and "one atrocious trumpet."
They had played at the county jail, the workhouse, the
community center, and a few PTA meetings. Soon after,
the unit was dissolved.

But such failures were rare. When the project began,
there were only eleven recognized symphony orchestras in
the United States. At its height, the WPA created thirty-
four more, from one end of the country to the other. In
the metropolitan centers it was no surprise, for music and
musicians had flourished there before the Depression. But
in cities where symphonies were unknown and no one had
realized there was any demand for such music, it was
astonishing to find that WPA funds and energy could

build enduring orchestras so swiftly. The WPA symphony orchestras of Oklahoma and Utah are but two such examples.

New York City, which boasted the Philharmonic, found room for two new WPA symphony orchestras. What they accomplished, giving concerts at low admission prices, was described by Daniel Gregory Mason, professor of music at Columbia University:

> They have vastly deepened qualitatively, as well as broadened quantitatively, our musical public. People either go to these concerts to enjoy music itself, or they stay away. . . . The audiences at New York University's Sunday evening concerts were . . . a revelation. Seventeen hundred people, the capacity of the hall, would be seated half-an-hour before the concert began, hundreds more remained outside, unable to get in. These people gave breathless attention to the music, never coughing or moving restlessly about . . . and stayed until it ended. You could see that for them the music was a thing of beauty and deep appeal. . . . To hear and see such audiences filled one with a renewed confidence of our musical destiny.

The Madrigal Singers were one of the most accomplished choral groups created on the music project. It was the idea of Lehman Engel, a young musician who had come up from Mississippi in 1929 to study at the Juilliard School. He had made a phenomenal name in music circles for his compositions. By twenty-four, he had written an opera, five pieces for Martha Graham's dance company, and the music for Sean O'Casey's Broadway play, *Within the Gates*, all the while conducting several amateur choral groups. Invited to join the Federal Music Project of New

York (on a nonrelief basis) he formed the Madrigal
Singers:

> I had recently discovered English madrigals for myself,
> and this gave me the chance to work with them. Out
> of some 100 relief applicants I picked eight men and
> eight women. Their ages ranged from about 30 to 60,
> and all had had some professional experience. The WPA
> gave us an extraordinary opportunity. Where else could
> you rehearse a choir two and a half hours every week-
> day, paying them for it?
> Our first concert was at a Harlem Y. Only fifteen
> people showed up. But we persisted, eager to sing any-
> where. We got good reviews from the beginning and
> before long we were giving concerts at the New School,
> Town Hall, and Carnegie Hall as well as in settlement
> houses. Our admission charge was 25 cents. The singers
> got the usual $23.86 a week. We did at least 80 con-
> certs a year until we disbanded in 1939. Our repertory
> grew rapidly to take in the Renaissance and Baroque
> music of England, France, Spain, Germany, the Nether-
> lands, Italy, and finally we were doing contemporary
> music, too. We performed the works of Charles Ives,
> which gave me the rare privilege of getting to know him.

Engel worked with the Federal Theatre, too, composing
the music for *Murder in the Cathedral* and conducting
the orchestra for *The Cradle Will Rock* through its rehearsals up to that memorable night when it was dropped
by the project and Blitzstein's piano was substituted for
the orchestra.

Composers as well as performers were encouraged and
supported by the Federal Music Project. Funds were raised
to commission composers to write specific works. But the

WPA's most signal contribution was the Composers Forum Laboratory. Originated on the New York project by Ashley Pettis, it ran for five years. The object was to stimulate the development of American composition by giving the creators the first serious chance to hear their work performed. The composer submitted his new work to a committee of prominent musicians and project leaders. Accepted work was scheduled for rehearsal, to which the composer was invited. If he chose, he could conduct his own work and even provide the performing artists. After the new music was performed, the audience would offer comments and ask questions about the composer's work and contemporary music, and the composer would reply from the platform.

The innovation spread—soon the music projects in Boston, Philadelphia, Chicago, and Los Angeles were conducting similar forum laboratories. Transcripts of the discussions in New York and Boston were made and copies filed with the Library of Congress. Musicologists can find out now what Aaron Copland, William Schuman, Roy Harris, and some sixty other composers thought of the music they were composing back in the thirties. The composers also took part in discussions of contemporary music with hundreds of WPA music teachers.

The creation of an Index of American Composers was another service the project undertook. The researchers prepared an alphabetical list of composers, with extensive information on their life, work, and performances; an alphabetical list of compositions arranged by form; program notes with excerpts from reviews; and finally, notes on the derivations of folk tunes, legends, and settings. Although the Index was neither completed nor published, the card files are accessible in the music division of the Library of Congress. They record more than 7,000 compositions by over 2,200 native and resident American composers.

The retraining of music teachers on relief was one of the goals of the project. To avoid competing with self-supporting private teachers, lessons were given only to those unable to pay. But music education on the WPA went far beyond that. At one point the project employed 6,000 music teachers. They reached almost 14 million pupils, many of whom had never had music instruction in any form. The WPA offered classes in composition, theory, appreciation, history, and conducting choral or instrumental groups. It gave group instruction in folk dancing and folk music to both children and adults. It provided the opportunity for community groups to enjoy self-expression through voice and instrument.

In Mississippi alone, the project reached 70,000 people across forty counties, evoking such an intense response to music that the sale of secondhand pianos shot up. South Carolina pleaded for "fifty times as many teachers" as the project could supply. In Maine, where only CCC boys made up the first classes, the local people considered music lessons a joke. Soon they were crowding into the teacher's farmhouse to learn what they were missing. The WPA teachers in Taos County, New Mexico, went to the rural schools to give the first music lessons ever taught in those communities.

To build music into the life of such communities the WPA offered programs in public schools, hospitals, welfare institutions, parks, and playgrounds. It sponsored amateur orchestras and children's rhythm bands, choruses and glee clubs. Almost anyone within reach of a WPA unit who wanted to learn something about music was given the chance. In New York City over 15,000 people (ages six to seventy-five) attended WPA music classes each week. They could choose among dozens of different courses. The human value of the Federal Music Project is reflected in this report from New York:

> If one thinks of hordes of people flocking to these free classes for a superficial smattering of music knowledge, even a cursory visit to these centers would soon shatter this belief. A student coming for a slight knowledge of piano, voice, or violin, soon discovers that he does not "belong." Correlated theoretical subjects are an integral part of the curricula. He must learn to listen, to analyze, even to create, as well as play. The seriousness of the students is their outstanding characteristic. . . .
>
> Students have ample opportunity to bring their work before audiences in the student assemblies, which range from soloists in all instruments and voice to choral and orchestral groups. Recently students from the Central Manhattan School in Harlem gave a concert in the 135th Street YMCA which, in addition to soloists and chorus, had an orchestra of 37 pieces, made up of youths ranging from 8 or 10 to 17 or 18 years of age. The instruments were none too good, but a Brahms Hungarian Dance was performed with an esprit which evoked wild acclaim, and deservedly. . . .
>
> When there was a possibility of Midtown Community Music Center being closed recently, a flood of letters poured in to the administrative offices of the Music Project. A typical letter reads: "In these days of distress and depression when all avenues of endeavor have been closed to us, either for reason good or bad, this chance to thus occupy our enforced leisure has spelled the difference between sanity and the blackest despair. It has maintained our morale and given us strength and hope

to carry on until happier times shall once more come back."

The music project was a part of the joint committee on the folk arts set up by the WPA to gather and preserve folk material. With a sound truck, Herbert Halpert made his way through the South, from the Virginias to the Carolinas, Georgia, Florida, Mississippi, and Louisiana, collecting old songs and melodies. He accumulated 419 twelve-inch acetate recordings on his Southern expedition. Later he made ten more recordings of the urban folk music of New York City. (These are all deposited in the folk song archives of the Library of Congress. They can be heard at the Record Section of the Music Division.) The project cooperated with other agencies and institutions to collect folk music in New Mexico—songs and tunes whose origins went back to Spain, Cuba, and Mexico. In Mississippi, the project gathered black work and play songs, spirituals, river songs, and fiddler's tunes. The Oklahoma project made over 300 recordings of the songs and dances of five Indian tribes, as well as a portfolio of transcribed fiddle tunes. In Louisiana, Creole and Acadian songs were collected; in North Carolina, a rich variety of black music —spirituals, shouts, blues, jubilees, work songs; in the Virginias, music of the mountains; in California, the songs from the days of the Spanish missions and the Gold Rush.

At first it had been feared that WPA music teachers could not be relied upon to research folk music in a professional way. But their field work proved that they could meet high academic standards. The fact that they gathered the music in their own territory gave them a great advantage over outsiders. The people who created and transmitted such music felt at home with these neighbors, and the results were all the more authentic.

11 LITERARY SHARECROPPERS

In "normal" times—whatever those are—the writer has three ways in which to support himself and his family. He may pay his bills entirely by writing, he may have a job and write in his spare time, or he may have been lucky enough, through inheritance or marriage, to come into enough money so that he need not worry about royalties.

Few writers have been able to find the right parents or mates to fall into the last category. The majority have had to rely on jobs for a living, leaving writing for their spare time. But "most jobs in this country," as the author Elmer Davis once pointed out, "are apt to leave a man too tired to do very good work after his day's work is over—especially as the jobs most congenial to people with a bent for writing are apt to be writing jobs, which leave a man tired of writing by dinner time, and not in the best condition to begin writing what he lovingly regards as his good stuff, after dinner."

Recognizing this, some writers have avoided jobs in journalism, radio, television, theater, films, publishing, advertising, and public relations. They've chosen jobs remote from writing, such as farming, taxi driving, carpentry, and storekeeping. A good many have taken up teaching. But again, as Mr. Davis observed, "almost all of us have found, if we attained any success as writers, that sooner or later we had to quit the job or quit writing."

And what of the author, the man or woman who hopes to make a living by his or her trade? Writing books simply does not pay—for all but a handful. Has it ever?

In Malcolm Cowley's 1954 study, *The Literary Situation*, he concluded that "authors as a class were replaceable persons who received only a minute portion of the wealth they helped to create. . . . Aside from the hard-working authors of textbooks, standard juveniles, mysteries, and Westerns, I doubt that two hundred Americans earned the major portion of their incomes, year after year, by writing hard-cover books."

Toward the end of the thirties, David Cohn, a Southern writer whose books got fine reviews but had modest sales, compared his situation with the tenant farmer who was always in debt to the plantation store:

He is a cotton sharecropper, I am a literary sharecropper. Each of us, by virtue of the system, has a certain amount of economic security even if it is at a low level. His employer, the planter, and my employer, the publisher, must keep us alive so that we may create cotton and books by the sales of which they earn their livelihood. If he gets an advance of fifteen dollars a month so that he can eat and clothe himself while he is making a crop, I get a lump sum advance so that I can eat and clothe myself while I am writing a book. In both cases, whether by calculation or coincidence, the advance always seems to be just enough to keep body and soul within hailing distance of each other.

During this period, Malcolm Cowley found his own experience to be similar. In 1929 his first book of poems, *Blue Juniata*, gained critical approval but earned only a bit above his advance of $125. Poetry didn't sell well then (and not much better now). The first edition of his important literary history, *Exile's Return*, appeared in 1934 and barely earned the advance of $350.

The situation did not change much in the next thirty years. Benjamin Appel published fourteen novels between 1934 and 1963. "None sold over 5000 copies," he said, "and my financial mainstay has been paperbacks, juveniles, and quite often a working wife."

During the Great Depression the mainstay for writers was the government. There was nothing new about writers working for the government. They had been doing it for a long time: Nathaniel Hawthorne, our consul in Liverpool; Washington Irving, our ambassador to Spain; Herman Melville, customs officer in the Port of New York; William Dean Howells, consul in Venice; James Russell Lowell, ambassador to Great Britain. But when the Federal Writers Project was launched, for the first time in American history writers began working for the government as writers.

One of them was Alexander Crosby. In 1936 he was editor of the Paterson *Press*, a weekly newspaper started by the printers who had long been on strike against the daily papers of Paterson, New Jersey. The strikers had high hopes of building their weekly into a daily, but their circulation was too small and the paid advertising insufficient. There wasn't enough money to pay both the printer and the editorial staff. So the editor was fired.

Crosby found a job on the Federal Writers Project of New Jersey. The pay offered was about what the paper had given him, "and in that year of the depression," he

Craftsmen recorded 20,000 pieces of American decorative art for the Index of American Design, a nationwide WPA art project. *WPA Photo No. 69-N-22577 in the National Archives*

The WPA operated art centers throughout the country, teaching people of all ages, but especially the young. *WPA Photographs, Archives of American Art, Smithsonian Institution*

WPA poster-makers helped draw people into all the activities of the Federal Arts Projects. *The Museum of the Performing Arts, The New York Public Library*

"BATTLE HYMN"

a new play about
JOHN BROWN of
HARPER'S FERRY
By
MICHAEL BLANKFORT
and MICHAEL GOLD

at the
EXPERIMENTAL
THEATRE: W. 63D ST.
east of Broadway
FEDERAL THEATRE
evenings only 8:40
admission
25¢ to 55¢
CI. 7-5855

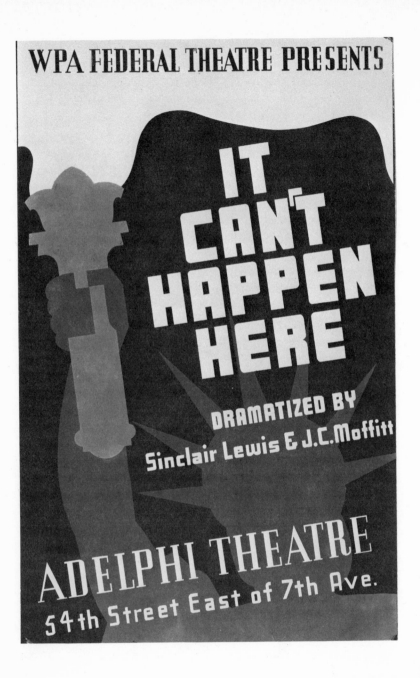

said, "it seemed positively wonderful. I would not suffer through weeks or months of unemployment, stalling on the rent and other bills, borrowing from friends, making promises to pay and then breaking most of them."

He went to work in the state headquarters of the Federal Writers Project—an abandoned police station in Newark. He was twenty-nine. With five years' experience on a suburban daily as a reporter and news editor, he was put in charge of preparing the New Jersey state guidebook.

The staff on which he depended was of uneven quality: a veteran newsman who could turn out 5,000 words a day, but few of them to Crosby's standard; two excellent women, one an expert on civic affairs and the other a poet; a former writer for the *Wall Street Journal*; an author of children's stories; and "a delightful Irishman who could never be described as a former drinker." The rest were "an assortment of unemployed persons from a variety of occupations, none of them connected with a typewriter."

The Newark staff was reinforced by workers in eight district offices around the state. Each district collected historical and other data about the counties in its area. Crosby found that only a small part of what they sent in was usable in the state guide.

The idea of putting unemployed writers to work preparing guidebooks came from several sources almost at the same time. The Authors League of America—the country's oldest professional organization of writers—had suggested it to Washington early in 1934. It proposed that the government hire writers to make "a survey of varying aspects of everyday life as it is lived in all parts of the United States." The League thought at least 500 jobless writers could be found for such useful work. From newsmen, too, came pressure for projects to report various relief activities. As a result, unemployed writers, photographers, clerks, and typists were hired to provide public information on the WPA. In the spring of 1935 a coalition of twenty-three organizations representing these unemployed professionals and white-collar workers met in New York to rally public support for a federal job program.

Several people pointed out that there had been no comprehensive guide to the United States since the revised Baedeker book of 1909. Americans traveled more by car than the rest of the world put together, yet where was there an up-to-date directory to show them what was worth seeing? With Americans spending billions a year on travel, wouldn't the expense of getting out good state and national guides be justified?

When the writers project was established as part of Federal One, two questions had to be answered: Who would be eligible to work on it? and, What should they do? Ignoring aesthetic issues, the authorities ruled that any kind of a writer who was on relief would be eligible. That meant poets, novelists, journalists, advertising and publicity writers, historians, biographers, technical writers— wordsmiths in general. And they need not be experienced. It was made clear that so long as they were on relief, young college men and women who loved writing were welcome to apply.

The nonfiction people were vastly in the majority. That helped the planners decide that an informational program would make the greatest use of the diverse skills the project could muster.

It was fortunate that the project's chief was Henry G. Alsberg. Jerre Mangione, one of his chief assistants, wrote:

No one, not even Alsberg, had ever contended he was a talented administrator. His chief value as a director was his intuitive understanding of what the Project was capable of doing, within the limitations of its personnel, and his steadfast devotion to the high editorial standards that made the American Guide series a treat instead of a bore.

Alsberg, then fifty-seven, had been on Hopkins' staff for a year. Born in New York of German-Jewish parentage, he had taken a law degree at Columbia, quit the bar to study literature at Harvard, then gone into journalism. He covered Europe for years, including the Russian Revolution, then helped administer relief to Russia's famine victims. Back in the United States, he protested the Communists' suppression of civil liberties, and continued to fight for social justice. He edged into the off-Broadway theater by successfully adapting S. Ansky's famous Yiddish play, *The Dybbuk*, and then became a director of the Provincetown Playhouse in Greenwich Village. In 1934 he was appointed to an editorial post in one of the New Deal agencies.

When he was head of the writers project and its 6,500 employees, Alsberg's inability to make decisions led to many mistakes. Nevertheless, said Mangione, no one could deny "his inventive mind, his encyclopedic fund of knowledge, and his literary taste." His most important quality was his deep faith in people. Mangione, who observed him daily, describes him:

Fumbling constantly for cigarettes (and sometimes for Bisodol), spilling ashes and food over his clothing, Alsberg looked more like an absent-minded patriarch than an executive. Yet the craggy landscape of his brown face (absurdly interrupted by a square mustache golden with nicotine) together with his ponderous body and the rumbling Old Testament sound of his voice somehow combined to emit a steady current of authority.

Alsberg leaned especially on two men, Reed Harris, a young journalist who seemed a born administrator, and George W. Cronyn, a middle-aged novelist and college professor who took charge of the editorial work. Three of the key field supervisors were Joseph Gaer, an energetic Russian immigrant who had published widely; Lawrence Morris, formerly of the *New Republic* staff; and Katharine Kellock, an experienced traveler who had written for newspapers and magazines and who pressed hard for quality in the guidebooks. As tours editor, she supervised more than half the total wordage in all the state guidebooks.

The toughest job was to find the right man or woman for state directorships. The pay was low: $1,800 to $3,800, with most salaries at the lower end of the scale. Still, as Alsberg learned, "it is astonishing how many people whose names are in *Who's Who* will take a job of this sort because of present depression conditions." Most of the state directors chosen had been either college teachers, free-lance writers, or journalists.

Ideally a state director should have the combined qualities of diplomat, administrator, artist, and encyclopedist. Few had all those virtues, and many had none. Complicating the state director's task was his relationship with the state WPA administrator. These officials, mostly hard-boiled politicians, saw the Federal One jobs as opportunities for patronage. They did not like to work with someone who took orders directly from Washington rather than from them. Worse, they tended to view all the arts projects as crazy New Deal experiments that soon would, and ought to, die. That attitude often produced obstruction, interference, or total neglect.

Nevertheless, an enormous amount of work was accomplished. As W. T. Couch, Alsberg's regional director for the South, put it, "that good guide books were finally produced and published is little short of miraculous."

12 UNCOVERING AMERICA

The 1930s, as one historian has described them, were "a golden age of literary sociology. America had discovered itself to be a fascinating subject for exploration, dissection, and horrified if hopeful contemplation."

Going over the country inch by inch for its series of guidebooks, the Federal Writers Project made one of the richest contributions of that age. Lewis Mumford wrote:

> Of all the good uses of adversity, one of the best has been the conception and execution of a series of American guidebooks, the first attempt, on a comprehensive scale, to make the country itself worthily known to Americans. . . . Future historians will turn to these guidebooks as one who would know the classic world must still turn to Pausanias' ancient guidebook to Greece.

The WPAers, deep into the task of putting out the guides, could not foresee such praise from on high. When

Alexander Crosby took over editing the New Jersey guide, he found the file cabinets crowded with material:

> Many of these manuscripts had been submitted to the national editors at Washington, who had to pass on every sentence. There were literally hundreds of letters from Washington about hundreds of manuscripts, and there were hundreds and hundreds of carbon copies of the various drafts. Only one thing was missing: a method of labelling, so that the latest draft of any essay could be readily identified. True, many drafts bore the notation "revised." But when three different drafts of the essay on "Transportation and Communication" were all labeled "revised" which was the latest? The editorial staff often found themselves working on an obsolete draft, or wasting time trying to figure out which draft was which. There was an easy solution. I ordered the typists to put a date on every page of every manuscript. Looking back, that may have been my greatest contribution to the production of the state guide.

Crosby, who had hired three young veterans of his New Jersey labor paper when it finally collapsed, ran into another problem—censorship. His new men had not only skills but a bent for muckraking that worried the national editors in Washington:

> Our manuscripts told how Seabrook Farms had used teargas against the striking farm workers, how RCA manufactured clubs for strikebreakers at its Camden factory, and—from the consumer standpoint—how trichinosis was spread from the meat of garbage-fed hogs. All of this material was killed in Washington,

which finally sent an order that the words "teargas" and "trichinosis" were not to be used in the New Jersey guide.

It seemed to be the policy of the Washington editors to tone down anything that looked controversial. We quietly adopted a policy of our own. In handling controversial topics, write as strongly as possible. Washington could then edit the manuscript, softening it to a degree, but leaving it stronger than if we had written timorously.

The same desire to be frank about the past evoked violent attack on the Massachusetts guide when it appeared in 1937. A Boston reporter running through the 675-page book found that forty-one lines were devoted to the case of Sacco and Vanzetti, the immigrant anarchists whose trial and execution in the 1920s had aroused worldwide protest. The front-page story, headlined SACCO VANZETTI PERMEATE NEW WPA GUIDE, was grabbed up by a press hostile to the New Deal. Editorials smeared the writers project with charges of communism. Burn the book and purge the writers! The heat intensified when other critics discovered that the guide took an anti-Establishment view of the Boston police strike (1919), the Lawrence textile strike (1912), and child labor.

The hoopla had the predictable effect of censorship in Boston. Houghton Mifflin's first edition of 10,000 copies sold out, and the guide went into a second and a third printing. Neither Harry Hopkins nor FDR took the unfavorable publicity seriously. But Alsberg became nervous and ordered his field officers "to curb extreme outbursts of indignation at social injustice." There was nothing extreme about the disputed passages, however. They were accurate and truthful. They were legitimate interpretations of historical facts. So were the passages in the New Jersey guide that had alarmed the Washington editors.

By the spring of 1937, the project began to show impressive results. First came the Idaho state guidebook, then guidebooks to Washington, D.C., and all of the six New England states, and, by the end of the year, *Cape Cod Pilot*, a deliciously personal stroll up that sandy arm of Massachusetts.

The Idaho book, the project's pioneer, was almost a one-man effort by its state director, the novelist Vardis Fisher. Working for months without an office, then confined to a single dirty room with only one typewriter and two desks for his staff of ten (who proved to be almost useless), Fisher nevertheless turned in a completed guidebook ahead of his racing competitors. His success in reaching the finishing line first was an embarrassment to the national office. Other states had infinitely greater resources to draw upon—how could Fisher have done it? And not only written it almost alone, but gotten it published locally by Caxton Press! Simply by giving free rein to his artistry and individualism. He ignored the mass of contradictory directives from Washington and did what he thought right. He completed the 405-page book in ten months doing not only most of the writing but the touring and logging of all the state's roads. His work was hailed by the historian Bruce Catton as not only a comprehensive and readable guide but "a bit of literature worth reading for its own sake." *The New York Times* said it was a credit to "one of the most powerful imaginative writers of our day."

Three months later, the guide to *Washington: City and Capital*, appeared. Its huge size alone was enough to make a big impression on those congressional skeptics accus-

tomed to baiting the project. Not only were the glories of
the capital described, but also the garbage of its ghetto.
Sterling A. Brown, the Howard University professor and
poet, wrote the section dealing with black life in Washington. He indicted white power for keeping blacks in
virtual enslavement down to the days of the WPA. It was
a blunt treatment of an explosive issue to appear under
government imprint.

Cape Cod Pilot was signed by a Jeremiah Digges, which
turned out to be the pen name of Josef Berger, a writer
who had scratched for a living in Provincetown since 1934.
When he got a job on the writers project, he was allowed
to work at home preparing a section on Cape Cod for the
Massachusetts guide. He had already written most of an
unconventional guide to the Cape under contract to a
local publisher. A few months later he finished it in time
left over from WPA duties. Project supervisors argued
him into letting it appear as a WPA guide. In return, he
was allowed to keep whatever royalties the book might
earn. *Time* called the book "the boldest and best" of all
the guide series. One critic said he "never expected to read
a guidebook through word for word."

The success of *Pilot* helped Berger win a Guggenheim
Fellowship, and he quit his WPA job. Later, remembering
the desperate plight of his family in those early Depression
years, he said, "If the Project had not come along, just as
I was at the end of my rope, I would have had to abandon
the profession I had been trained to do."

Mapping and describing the road tours within a state
was one of the more pleasurable aspects of the work.
Crosby enjoyed it so much he assigned himself to six of
the forty-six New Jersey tours, and wrote parts of most
of the others. He said:

To write a tour well, you had to drive slowly and keep your eyes open. The best plan was to have another editorial worker as a driver so you could forget about traffic and make notes on the countryside. What was the name of the stream you just crossed, and at what point on the odometer did you cross it? Where does a side road go? How do people make a living in the various towns? What crops are grown in the fields? Does an interesting old house have a history worth telling?

Crosby did not think all the tour descriptions were as good as they could have been. There wasn't time and manpower enough to dig in deep. For instance, the staff could rarely examine the files of old newspapers—a gold mine of local history. Crosby's Aunt Phoebe, whom he introduced to the swamps of south New Jersey in 1937, fell in love with them and (in a touch of nepotism) wrote the introduction to Tour 35 in the book, which runs from Ship Bottom to where the present state routes 70 and 72 now meet. She kept returning to the spot year after year, until she died at the age of ninety.

In 1942, when the writers project ended, 51 major volumes in the "American Guide" series had been published, as well as 30 guides to major cities, 20 guides on specialized subjects such as Death Valley and the Oregon Trail, and 150 books in a "Life in America" series. Even more numerous were the WPA books and pamphlets which put small-town America under the historical and geographical microscope.

The state guides all have a common pattern. The first part contains essays on the historical, social, and cultural life of the state; the second examines the cities in the same way, as well as their major points of interest; and the last part—usually about half of each volume—logs the roads that crisscross the state, enriching each mile with tidbits about the past and present. Maps, illustrations, a calendar of annual events, an historical chronology, and an index continue to make the guides useful more than a generation later.

The WPA guides belong to what the critic Alfred Kazin has called that "literature of nationhood" which began with the documentation of America in the Depression. In his study of prose literature, *On Native Grounds*, Kazin made this evaluation of what the project had done:

The WPA state guides, seemingly only a makeshift, a stratagem of administrative relief policy to tide a few thousand people along and keep them working, a business of assigning individuals of assorted skills and interests to map the country, mile by mile, resulted in an extraordinary contemporary epic. Out of the need to find something to say about every community and the country around it, out of the vast storehouse of facts behind the guides—geological, geographic, meteorological, ethnological, historical, political, sociological, economic—there emerged an America unexampled in density and regional diversity.

Were the state guides, as some felt, only a project for research workers rather than for writers? Perhaps; but the literary merit of some of them was greater than most people have appreciated, and their coverage of the country anything but mechanical. More than any other literary form in the thirties, the WPA writers' project, by illustrating how much so many collective skills could do to uncover the collective history of the country, set the tone of the period. As the first shock and panic of the depression passed, and the social reporters settled down to cover the country with a growing interest in the epic unfolding of their investigations, the WPA guides became something more than a super-Baedeker . . . [they] became a repository as well as a symbol of the reawakened American sense of its own history.

Some of the WPA writers felt that way while they were on the job. "Without doubt," Crosby said recently, "my two years on the Writers Project were the most interesting of my working life. Despite the misfits and the do-nothings, we had enough good workers to produce one of the best of the state guides. I loved the job."

But not everyone would agree. Some of the people on the writers project thought the guidebooks were only hackwork. (They did not anticipate that in the 1970s about twenty-five of the state guidebooks would still be in print.) Were tour guides what a poet or novelist should be writing? Why couldn't they be allowed to develop their talent like people on the Federal Art Project, who were painting and sculpting what they wished, and signing their own names to their work? If the artists were given a wall to paint a mural, shouldn't the WPA just as logically supply writers with paper and printing for literary magazines?

While pressing for that opportunity, project writers banded together here and there to publish their own literary work in mimeographed form. In San Francisco they put out a hundred pages of poems, stories, essays, and excerpts from plays and novels, calling it "Material Gathered." From Nebraska came "Shucks"; from Vermont, "The Catamount." Stimulated by these private ventures, Alsberg convinced Viking Press to publish a book, *American Stuff*, to which fifty project writers contributed.

Why didn't the writers project do more of this? Why

did it confine its workers to nonfiction during their office hours? For two basic reasons, according to Jerre Mangione: "the fear that if writers were allowed to work on their own subjective efforts Congress and public opinion would soon put the Project out of business; and the preponderance of Project employees who, though able to function as researchers or editors, had little or no talent for imaginative writing."

Talent was there, some of it among the best America has known. Take these names, a sampling from the writers project roster: Saul Bellow, Nelson Algren, Richard Wright, Isaac Rosenfeld, Kenneth Fearing, Edward Dahlberg, William Gibson, Kenneth Rexroth, Conrad Aiken, Margaret Walker, Jack Conroy, Weldon Kees, Willard Motley, Vincent McHugh, Norman MacLeod, Harry Roskolenko, Jerre Mangione, Ralph Ellison, Harold Rosenberg, Studs Terkel, George Willison, Sterling Brown, John Cheever, Loren Eiseley, Saul Levitt, Paul Corey, Benjamin Botkin, Vardis Fisher.

Naturally, such writers were usually on the big-city projects—New York, Chicago, Boston, San Francisco. It was the metropolitan centers that drew hopeful writers from all parts of the country. Most of them were young in the thirties; few had yet built any reputation. Nelson Algren was one of the rare ones who had already published a novel (*Somebody in Boots*). He spent four years on the Illinois project. What did the WPA do for him? In a taped interview with H. E. F. Donohue he said:

. . . it was very good. . . . It served to humanize people who had been partially dehumanized. There had been, I believe, in those years between 1929, 1930, '31, when people had been self-respecting, lost their self-respect by being out of work and then living by themselves began to feel the world was against them. To such people the WPA provided a place where they began to communicate with people again. They got a little self-respect back, and, I know it put me in touch with people again, and it also put me in touch with people who were politically alert. . . .

Algren, like most of the writers on the project, was paid $23.86 a week. He was expected to put in thirty hours for those wages and to produce between 1,200 and 2,000 words a week (a standard many supervisors ignored). That left writers ample time and energy to do their own creative work, if they wished.

William Gibson, the playwright, was one of the younger writers who managed to get started while on the WPA. In his autobiography, *A Mass for the Dead*, he tells how. A Bronx boy, he had dropped out twice from City College, worked briefly as a waiter-pianist at a lake resort, run messages in the downtown skyscraper district, tried learning auto mechanics in a trade school, peddled mops and pails door-to-door, and then subsided into home relief at the age of twenty-one. On the strength of a single short story published (for free) in a British quarterly, he got on the writers project—only to find himself shunted into the Historical Records Section. The work turned into a dismal "inventory of garbage and gas permits issued in bygone days."

He served out each day amid the storage bins of the damp cellars of municipal buildings and then went to a tiny office he rented halfway between job and home. He saved every penny he could from his pay, and whenever he had piled up about $75, he would tell his WPA supervisor he had a temporary job "in private industry" and devote a month's leave to writing. He finished a play that was not good enough for Broadway production, but which earned him a chance to apprentice to the Barter Theater in Virginia in the summer of 1939. He never went back to the WPA and never held a regular job again. Gibson got nothing from the project but the chance to stay alive while learning to write on his own time. Maybe that was enough.

The climate in which WPA writers worked was stormy. Alsberg's executive secretary, Dora Thea Hettwer, complained that "the number of workers . . . changed continually. Just after any election the quotas were all reduced and everyone fought for his life. How we produced worthwhile books is a mystery. Pink slips [dismissal notices] and attacks from Congress kept us all in jitters. We were always on the griddle."

Attacks on budgets were matched by constant attacks on political beliefs. The press hammered relentlessly at the project for sheltering radicals and providing them with vehicles for propaganda. Investigations by local, state, and federal agencies were demoralizing to the writers. They were accused of inserting into manuscripts "appeals to class hatred" and "inflammatory" references to "underprivileged" or "downtrodden" black people.

Still Mangione was able to say that he and other WPAers

. . . felt we had never done anything of more value in our lifetime and suspected that it would be difficult if not impossible to ever find again a method of earning a living that could involve us so wholly and selflessly. Notwithstanding the dismaying confusion that attended nearly everything we did, we had the sense of being part of a significant historical event. In a literal sense, we *were* making history, for nothing like the Writers' Project or the other three federal arts projects had ever been tried by any nation anywhere.

13 FOLK LIFE IN BLACK AND WHITE

Something new began for black people with the election of FDR. Presidents before him had occasionally asked advice from black leaders. But now, for the first time, blacks entered federal agencies in increasing numbers. Highly trained men and women took part as advisers in race relations and soon showed that they could do far more. Called the "Black Cabinet," they pressed in every possible way for economic and political equality. Their prime goal was jobs in government and industry on the basis of ability and training—not color.

As a result, about 26 percent of the workers on WPA projects in the South were black. In the country as a whole, about 16 percent were black. In the South, they were paid less than whites, but even their lowest pay rate was higher than most blacks were earning from private industry. The WPA gave jobs to black professional and white-collar workers, too. Actors, artists, musicians, and writers were among those able to use their talent and skills, especially on the big-city projects. By 1939, more than a million blacks were earning their living from WPA.

Recalling those times, Horace Cayton, the black sociologist who headed a WPA research project, said:

In spite of the Depression, there was hope. Great hope, even though the people suffered. To be without money is a disgrace in America today. The middle class looks upon welfare Negroes as morally corrupt because they haven't worked. But in the Depression, there were so many whites who were on relief. So the Negro would look, and he wouldn't see any great difference. Oh, there was a difference: a disproportion of Negroes on labor than on skilled jobs in WPA. But if Negroes were on relief, so were whites: we're gonna have a better day. That was the feeling. . . . You worked, you got a paycheck and you had some dignity. All the songs they used to have about WPA:

> I went to the poll line and voted
> And I know I voted the right way
> So I'm askin' you, Mr. President
> Don't take away this W P and A.

When they got on WPA, you know what they'd mostly do. First, buy some clothes. And tried to get a little better place to live. The third thing, was to get your teeth fixed. When you're poor you let your teeth go. . . . WPA . . . There was some humanity then. . . .

The writers project appointed Sterling A. Brown the national editor of Negro affairs and made the novelist and poet Arna Bontemps a supervisor in Chicago. Among other black writers on the project were Claude McKay, Richard Wright, William Attaway, Roi Ottley, Margaret Walker, Robert Hayden, Zora Neale Hurston, Frank

Yerby, Fenton Johnson, Ralph Ellison, and John H. Johnson (who later became publisher of *Ebony* and *Black
World* magazines).

Richard Wright was the son of an illiterate Mississippi
sharecropper. His formal schooling ended in the ninth
grade. He went to Chicago at the age of nineteen, where he
worked as porter, dishwasher, substitute postal clerk, insurance agent, hospital orderly, and street sweeper. Wright's
early poems and stories, published in radical magazines,
won attention. He joined a group of black writers who met
to read manuscripts and discuss craft problems. In 1936 he
left the relief rolls to join the WPA, first on the Federal
Theatre Project and soon on the Federal Writers Project,
where he met Nelson Algren.

According to Algren, Wright was the one whom the
project helped most. Algren said later, "He was more
alert to its advantages and more diligent than most of us.
He used the time it gave him to write 'Big Boy Leaves
Home' [a short story] and *Native Son* [the novel that later
became a huge critical and popular success]. Whether he
would have been able to write *Native Son* if he had had to
go on working at the post office is problematical. Surely it
would have been a much harder grind."

On the project, Wright's assignment was researching the
black history of Chicago and Illinois. He was one of forty
field workers digging up such facts for the Illinois guidebook. He went to the office twice a week to report his
findings and to get a new assignment. Late in 1936, Wright's
"Big Boy" story was published in the anthology *New Caravan*, and was highly praised. He was reclassified on the
WPA as a group coordinator at $115 a month.

In the spring of 1937, he left Chicago for New York, but
was unable to effect a transfer to the writers project there
until the end of the year. Meanwhile he became the Harlem

reporter for the *Daily Worker*. Back again on the WPA, he wrote the detailed, factual section on Harlem for the *New York City Guide* and the more comprehensive and interpretive chapter called "Portrait of Harlem" in *New York Panorama*. In 1938, Wright won *Story* magazine's $500 prize for the best work submitted by anyone on the writers project. When *Native Son* was published, its guaranteed success (it was the first novel by a black to be made a Book-of-the-Month Club selection), together with the award of a Guggenheim Fellowship he received, enabled Wright to quit the WPA.

Introduced to Wright by Langston Hughes, Ralph Ellison, with Wright's aid, got a job on the New York project in 1938. With the time and energy left him after WPA hours, Ellison wrote some stories and started a novel. (His *Invisible Man* is considered one of the most important novels of our time.) His WPA research assignments ranged from black history to urban folklore and famous trials. He stayed with the project for four years, until it closed in 1942.

The older, more experienced black writers also profited by their WPA jobs. The project gave them an anchor in a time of despair. Bontemps, for instance, published his third novel, *Drums at Dusk*, while on the WPA; McKay was able to use research gathered on the job for his book *Harlem: Negro Metropolis*; and Hurston issued three books while on the Florida project.

But even more significant was the impetus given to serious black studies by the writers project. There were many black writers who needed work, and Alsberg hoped to engage them in the task of depicting the role of blacks in American life. Sterling A. Brown, teacher, editor, poet, and critic, took charge, enlisting the aid of many black and white experts. His office gave advice, and it planned and edited material on black life. In addition to what appeared about blacks in the state and local guides, Brown's office saw to it that special studies were undertaken and published, such as *Drums and Shadows: Survival Studies among the Georgia Coastal Negroes* and *The Negro in Virginia*.

While Alsberg's national staff backed the work of Brown's office, on the local projects (North as well as South) blacks constantly struggled against discrimination and the threat of pink slips. As everywhere else, they were usually the last to be hired and the first to be fired.

The most valuable work in black studies was the gathering of interviews with ex-slaves. In a massive undertaking, about 300 WPA interviewers collected some 2,300 interviews with ex-slaves in seventeen states. The number interviewed is estimated to be about 2 percent of the total ex-slave population still alive at that time. About two-thirds of those interviewed were eighty or older; many were past ninety or a hundred. In 1865, at the time of Emancipation, the age of those interviewed had been from one to fifty. The slave experience they talked about was mainly that of childhood.

Lawrence D. Reddick was one of the people who did the most to launch the interviewing of ex-slaves. Teaching black history at Kentucky State College, he believed the truth about slavery and Reconstruction could not be fully known or understood "until we get the view as presented through the slave himself." That evidence had begun to appear as early as the eighteenth century, when the first American slave narratives were published. Between 1830 and the Civil War there were hundreds more of these autobiographical accounts by fugitive slaves, most of them issued by abolitionists who wanted to challenge the benevolent portrait of slavery drawn by its apologists.

The 1930s revived interest in accounts of slave life. Historians and sociologists recognized the number of ex-slaves was rapidly diminishing. Now was the time to get the testimony of those who still survived. Scholars such as W. E. B. DuBois and Carter G. Woodson were leaders of a new black generation contesting the old sympathetic view of slavery. People who had swallowed the planter's punch concocted by such white historians as Ulrich B. Phillips needed an emetic. There was a call for studies of slavery written from the standpoint of the slave.

The first attempts to secure interviews with ex-slaves were made in 1929 through independent projects at Fisk and other Southern universities. With the advent of the New Deal, Reddick, who had taken part in the work at Fisk, made a pilot interview study with federal support. When the writers project was launched, John A. Lomax, a white Southerner who had made great contributions to folklore research, was asked to direct Southern work in his field. He introduced the interview method of collecting folklore and life histories. This oral history technique was applied not only to the ex-slaves but to studies of pioneers in Texas and Kansas and to the people of the Southeastern states.

Although Brown's office urged the hiring of qualified black writers, Washington headquarters had no control over personnel policy in the states. The result was that several Southern states hired whites only. But in others—especially Arkansas, Florida, Louisiana, and Virginia—separate black units were established, whose energy was devoted chiefly to research in black culture.

The WPA collection of ex-slaves' reminiscences began sporadically in the South. A concerted regional effort was not made until April, 1937, when a sampling of interviews forwarded from the Florida project so impressed

John Lomax that he proposed this work be done on a systematic basis in all the Southern and border states. Lomax's instructions to the field insisted upon the importance of recording interviews exactly as given—with no censorship.

Lomax had no control over hiring or assignments, and the great majority of the interviewers were white. Their biases and methods violated sound interview procedure. The whites, as can be realized from the transcripts, were often patronizing, condescending, and sometimes insulting. The result could be stock responses, evasive answers, or compliant "yassuhs." Occasionally, white interviewers revealed both sensitivity and insight in their interview technique. In places like Florida, where the interviewers were black, the difference in results is evident. Answers were engaged, candid, direct. Deep feelings were openly expressed.

Objectively considered, the ex-slave interviews share the usual shortcomings of many historical sources. But, as the historian C. Vann Woodward wrote of them, they "nevertheless have an unusual character. Confusing and contradictory as they are, they represent the voices of the normally voiceless, the inarticulate masses whose silence historians are forever lamenting." The evidence they provide, he said, obliges historians to reexamine many old questions and assumptions about the work ethic of slaves, master-slave relationships, slave religion, slave attitudes toward white society, intermarriage, and the profound historical experiences of Emancipation and Reconstruction.

When the project interviewing ended early in 1939, the records lay unused in state archives. Benjamin A. Botkin, the folklorist who succeeded Lomax, had the interviews assembled in typescript and deposited in the Library of

Congress in 1941. In 1945 he published his own brief selection from them in the volume *Lay My Burden Down: A Folk History of Slavery*. Even though that book directed scholars' attention to the archives in Washington, until recently, historians tended to neglect them. Not until 1972 did a publisher (Greenwood) print a set of nineteen volumes containing both the WPA and the Fisk interviews. Since then, a careful search of WPA materials in Mississippi archives has turned up nearly 2,000 additional pages of ex-slave interviews, apparently never forwarded to Washington. Perhaps still more treasure remains to be discovered in other state files.

The state guides included folklore as well as material on black history and culture. Wherever they could, project workers traced the ethnic roots of American culture and the changes that developed in the transfer of cultures from one land to another. It soon became apparent that folklore deserved more than casual attention. Alsberg began to see the writers project as the organizing force for a nation-wide collection. John Lomax sent instructions to his field staff of amateur folklorists, demanding that the work be done to professional standards. He wanted them to go to original sources rather than to copy material from books. When Botkin took over, he stressed the use of oral sources and the need to dig into the fresh fields of urban and industrial folklore. In a paper on WPA folklore research, Botkin described the rich varieties of material his staff was finding:

In New England a regional collection is investigating the lives and lore of Connecticut clockmakers and munitions workers, Rhode Island fishermen and French-Canadian textile workers, Maine clam diggers, Vermont Welsh slate workers and Italian granite workers, and a half-dozen additional nationality and occupational types of Massachusetts. . . . Tales of railroading, brick-making, and steel mills from Chicago; tales of the Oklahoma oilfields, tales of the Montana and Arizona copper mines; tales of Southern textile mill workers and service occupations.

Meanwhile, we are not neglecting the lore of the more strictly rural folk, past and present—folk songs of the Cumberlands from Virginia; histories and lore of the Southern tenant farmer . . . of the Conchs and Latin colony of Florida; Negro spirituals and play-party songs from Alabama and South Carolina; Louisiana voodoo and Creole lore; stories and songs of the Creole pioneers of Indiana; Spanish-American folk songs from New Mexico; old timers' and tall tales from Iowa, Idaho and Washington.

Out of such harvesting came WPA books like *Idaho Lore* and *South Carolina Folk Tales.* The Nebraska project issued a series of thirty folklore pamphlets. Louisiana prepared *Gumbo Ya-Ya.* From the Virginia project's huge collection of folklore material (mostly unpublished to this day) a scholar was recently able to extract 2,600 folk songs and ballads.

Alsberg believed there were two reasons for publishing all types and forms of storytelling by minority and ethnic groups: "First, to give a comprehensive picture of the composite America—how it lives and works and plays—as seen through its folk story-tellers; second, by the richness of material and the variety of forms to prove that the art of story-telling is still alive and that story-telling is an art."

On the New York City project, a Living Lore unit was started. The idea was to study a cross section of urban

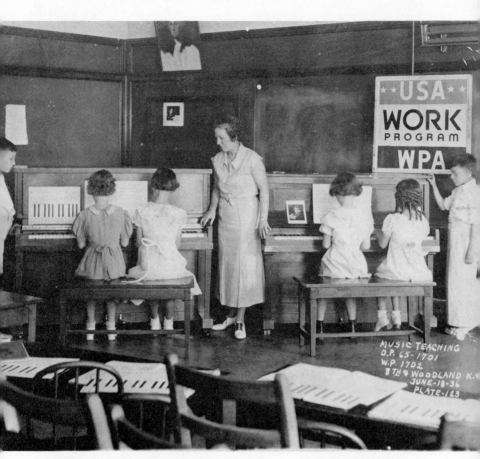

A WPA music teacher works with children in a Missouri community center. The Federal Music Project revived music as a communal art.
Culver Pictures

In a Harlem church a WPA instructor teaches eurythmic dancing. *Federal Writers Reporting Project and WPA Art Service, Municipal Archives of the City of New York*

The boys in a settlement house learn how to get out a weekly newspaper under the guidance of a WPA writer. *Art Service Project WPA, Municipal Archives of the City of New York*

The rich variety of work done by the Federal Writers Project is displayed in a hotel lobby. *Photographic Division, Federal Arts Project WPA, Municipal Archives of the City of New York*

Every time Congress threatened cuts in WPA funds the arts projects workers took to the picket line to fight for their jobs. *Wide World Photos*

folklore by occupational groups, tracing the links to nationality and neighborhood. There was no longer any doubt that industrial life in the city evolved its own folkways and its own fantasy patterns. The common element in the stories and anecdotes, in the voice rhythms and figures of speech of large groups of city dwellers, was occupation. How the WPA researcher went about his "creative listening" was described by one of the best of them, Hyde Partnow:

> The streets are full of people, some of them talking. You walk into a park and sit down on a bench. What do you listen for among the afternoon voices?
>
> . . . a man, drunk for the moment, is stumbling along the sidewalk. He goes for you, attaches himself, talks. You give him your ear. He keeps talking, won't let you go. . . . Why?
>
> Well, other things considered, maybe it's because you're a good listener. You give them plenty of time, you never laugh at the wrong time, you leave yourself out and, for the time being, you're willing to give in to them and, sitting or standing, look *out*, see, hear and— be silent. . . .
>
> We, on the folklore work, listen that way. One of our writers goes out with a shorthand pad, another with a typewriter. Both get lots of good folksay.
>
> I, myself, go out most of the time without any of the writer's firearms but my ears. After a while you get so sharp even your mother begins sounding like folk-say. Then you're all right, you're beginning to hear things.

This kind of folklore research was obviously more satisfying to writers than most of the other project assignments they might have had. It gave them a chance to learn about people and to grow in the use of their craft. Botkin served not only on the Federal Writers Project but also as president of the WPA Joint Committee on Folk Arts. When his official duties ended he published a dozen or more folklore anthologies, beginning with the enormously successful *Treasury of American Folklore*. He did more than anyone else to break folklore out of its mummy case and make it a popular part of American culture.

The ex-slave interviews and the Living Lore transcriptions were part of a literature of social exploration that emerged from that time of crisis. Americans felt a need to search out the truth about their lives. Documentary journalism sprang up, which gave them a sense of immediacy. There were teams who worked together with camera and typewriter to create documents of life in the thirties that are as vivid today as they were then. Dorothea Lange's and Paul Taylor's *An American Exodus*, Margaret Bourke-White's and Erskine Caldwell's *You Have Seen Their Faces*, and Walker Evans' and James Agee's *Let Us Now Praise Famous Men* are part of our heritage from this era.

Words alone could also produce penetrating social reports. There were Edmund Wilson's *The American Jitters*, Louis Adamic's *My America*, and James Rorty's *Where Life Is Better*. One of the most moving documents of this period was the writers project book *These Are Our Lives*, published in 1939. The WPA had already begun collecting the life stories of ex-slaves and of pioneers. But W. T. Couch, a regional director for the writers project envisioned using the life history technique to build a cross-sectional picture of Southern life. He began in his own state of North Carolina and extended the work into six other states. He knew that mountains of socioeconomic data about the South had been piled up. But sociology treated human beings as abstractions. He wanted to "let the people tell their stories. . . . This method of portraying the quality of life of a people, of revealing the real workings of institutions, customs, habits," he said, "has never before been used for the people of any region or country." Thousands of life histories were gathered by the project workers. Here, speaking their autobiographies, were black and white farmers—sharecroppers, tenants, laborers, owners—and people in the mill villages and factories, in service jobs and on relief. It was something new in social science, setting a precedent that many would follow. The historian Charles Beard said the book was "more powerful" than any novel he had ever read, and *The New York Times* described it as "history of a new and peculiarly honest kind."

Oral history is what they call it now. Use of the method grew slowly until 1950, when Columbia became the first university to open an oral history research office. Today there are more than 200 schools with professionally organized oral history operations, which has popularized the gathering of current social history with the tape recorder both by those inside and those outside academic circles.

What the Federal Writers Project began in the thirties has become one of the most useful tools for the advancement of knowledge in all fields. Millions of readers have been both informed and delighted by the extraordinary books edited from such oral materials. To cite just a few, there are Studs Terkel's *Division Street: America, Hard Times*, and *Working*, Theodore Rosengarten's *All God's Dangers: The Life of Nate Shaw*, Peter Joseph's *Good Times: An Oral History of the 1960s*, and Kenneth Lasson's *The Workers*.

14 PINK SLIPS

WPA must go on,
WPA must go on,
We won't take pink slips!
We won't take pink slips!

That sloganized lyric—sung to a syncopated beat, and accompanied often by a shuffle step—is imprinted indelibly on my mind. I shouted it, moaned it, chanted it, and bellowed it countless times on the picket line.

Pink-slip fever began raging in the blood almost the day I joined the Federal Theatre Project. Periodically, Washington would shower the arts projects with orders for dismissals. Only a few months after I was hired, pink slips were handed to sixteen of us on the New York publicity staff. My family could boast of constituting part of the 12.5 percent of the total number fired, for both my brother and I were on the list. We hit the pavement together, joined by a small army of pickets mustered by our union, the Workers Alliance. For two weeks we kept it up, until that batch of cuts was rescinded and we were back at our desks.

But protest didn't succeed in restoring jobs very often. In towns remote from the mass action the Workers Alliance could organize, WPAers felt isolated and helpless. On the writers project in Maine, a typist silently accepted her pink slip, went home to her cheap boardinghouse, and killed herself. When pink slips came again, that project's staff did its best to shore up the spirits of the victims by providing groceries until other jobs could be found.

"Organization and protest and demand alone held the Project together," said one of the New York writers, Earl Conrad. "It was all very precarious. We all had the feeling that if we didn't keep calling for the maintenance of the Project it would fold up."

The Workers Alliance, organized by the left wing in 1935 to fight for the needs of the unemployed, soon became, in many places, the official bargaining agency with the WPA. Its job actions were often joined by demonstrations of the Writers Union and the Artists Union.

This tradition of militant struggle went back to unionism's birth in the sweatshops, factories, railroads, and mines. Early in the New Deal, when a series of violent strikes shook the country again, it was revived.

In 1934, half a million textile workers struck in twenty states. Ten strikers were killed and hundreds were wounded in the successful effort to defeat the union. That same year, on the West Coast, longshoremen and maritime workers carried on an industrial battle that ended three months later in a partial victory. Two strikers were killed and hundreds were wounded.

In 1935, the CIO was established under the miners' leader, John L. Lewis, to organize the unorganized in the mass industries. In 1936, the CIO mounted its first offensive: It took on labor's mightiest enemies—the steel and auto industries—using mass picket lines, sit-ins, and sit-downs. The fervor of that organizing drive built up the fire we felt on the WPA projects. We were ready to do or die for human dignity, a decent living standard, and our democratic rights.

In the 1936 election, labor gave its wholehearted support to FDR for a second term, for, unlike many presidents before him, he had not used injunctions and troops to smash strikes. He won by a huge majority in a campaign in which he promised he had "just begun to fight" for more aid to the jobless. As one worker said, "Mr. Roosevelt is the only man we ever had in the White House who would understand that my boss is a sonofabitch."

But no sooner were the votes counted than word came from Washington for mass layoffs on the WPA. The order was to fire half a million. Nationally, over 8,000 workers on the arts projects were to be given pink slips. In New York City that meant nearly 2,000 people would go. The reason Hopkins gave was that WPA funds had been depleted to meet the drought emergency that summer. But actually Roosevelt wanted to limit the government's domestic deficit financing, and hoped—vainly—that private employers would now hire many of those still on the WPA.

The workers' reaction was dramatic. About 200 writers barricaded themselves into project headquarters, and a sit-down strike started on the theater project. I joined in. The police came in to throw us out, but every time they tried to lay a hand on us we sang "The Star-Spangled Banner" and they snapped to attention. When eleven dancers were arrested for disturbing the peace while picketing, labor and liberal organizations declared a boycott of WPA shows until workers fired for striking were reinstated. At local WPA headquarters on Columbus Avenue, 3,000 of us from all the projects started a mass demonstration.

The artists jammed into Miss McMahon's offices on East Thirty-ninth Street. One of the city WPA chiefs came in to threaten them with firing and a blacklist if they didn't leave at once. Desperate, they decided to sit in until Washington reversed itself. Enter the police. The artists formed a human chain against them. For an hour they fought bitterly with fists and nightsticks. One by one the artists were dragged out of the building. In the end, 219 artists were arrested; 12 artists and policemen needed medical care.

Our delegations picketed project chiefs at their homes and besieged Mayor Fiorello La Guardia in his office until he and the New York boss of WPA, Colonel Brehon Somervell, flew to Washington to discuss our case. Across the country, WPA workers took part in demonstrations and sit-ins, but the pink slips kept coming. In the fall of 1936 there had been 2.5 million workers on the WPA; a year later, there were fewer than 1.5 million.

The upheaval of that fall and winter did little to encourage art. The morale of the survivors was badly damaged. It was hard to do creative work, or even a routine job, when you could not be sure the job would be there tomorrow.

In the spring of 1937, the country pulled above the production levels of 1929. Roosevelt, excessively fearful of inflation, slashed government spending sharply. Congress reduced WPA funds by 25 percent—pink slips again for the WPA. In August, the economy suddenly cracked. All the gains made since 1935 were wiped out. In the next few months, 2 million people lost their jobs.

The cut in the WPA budget meant dropping 11,000 Federal One workers, 3,000 of them in New York alone. Of the 9,000 workers then on the New York arts projects, 7,000 went out on the streets in a work stoppage, but to no avail. (Even though in the New York art project files, to give but one example, there was a list of 2,000 needy artists waiting to be hired by the WPA.)

On a June morning, 2,248 Federal One workers in New York City got their pink slips. A fired clerk on the writers project tried to throw herself out the window. Hundreds of dismissed theater people stormed the project offices. Dancers on the Federal Music Project began a sit-down and hunger strike. Sixty workers barricaded themselves in at Federal One's payroll division, holding up paychecks for everyone still employed. In Philadelphia, St. Paul, and San Francisco, demonstrators took similar militant action.

But Washington wouldn't listen. There would be no compromise. As the summer passed, the demonstrations petered out. Congress had the final say—the power of the purse—and it showed no mercy.

Richard D. McKinzie, historian of the arts projects, explains why:

Because Federal One was so concentrated in a few congressional districts, the arts workers' plight and their disruptions failed to register with the national legislature as matters which required immediate attention and resolution. It is doubtful that congressmen or the President understood the issues behind the strike. The traditions of American bureaucracy militated against it. . . . Strikers had erred in thinking that if they pressed their immediate superiors hard enough, their superiors would agitate at the highest levels in Washington.

No, each administrator shielded the one above him, right up to the President. It would have taken a supplemental appropriation to reemploy those fired, and FDR had no intention of asking for one. Not only did he believe

Congress would never vote it, but he thought prosperity was returning and the need for federal relief would disappear.

He was wrong.

Worse was yet to come.

At home and abroad, liberal democracy was being challenged by fascism. Hitler had wiped out the republics of Central Europe without having to fire even one shot. He and Mussolini claimed they had put all their people to work providing their nations with both guns and butter. They sneered at American democracy for failing to end unemployment.

In America, native Fascists were organizing, winning an alarming number of followers. The Silver Shirts, Huey Long, the Black Legion, the German-American Bund, Father Coughlin and the Christian Front—all preached hatred of Jews, blacks, labor, and radicals. They found some support in Washington among those who feared a Roosevelt despotism and those who used that charge to cloak their opposition to his social welfare program.

The loudest voice from the right was now heard in the nation's capital. In 1938 Congress created the House Committee on Un-American Activities (HUAC), with Martin Dies, a Texas Democrat, as chairman. He made "the Communist menace" his rallying cry. The crisis of the thirties had been caused by a "conspiracy," he said. Ferret out the conspirators, and we'll soon be back to the good old days. Plenty of people believed him. They had suffered nine long years of the Depression, and maybe, they thought, Dies was right.

That summer of 1938, the Dies Committee began hearings. The homegrown Fascists were ignored. The "Reds" were the target. Witness after witness made undocumented charges of the wildest kind. Those accused were almost

never given the chance to reply. Within a week, hundreds
of organizations, newspapers, and unions had been
branded Communistic. The Boy Scouts, Camp Fire Girls,
Catholic groups—all were depicted as part of a Red network. Dozens of individuals—including actors, authors,
playwrights, directors—had their careers virtually ruined
on the basis of unsubstantiated charges presented at the
various HUAC hearings.

Observing the committee's behavior, Harold Ickes,
FDR's Secretary of the Interior, said of chairman Dies, "To
my mind, the most contemptible human being in public life
is the one who will recklessly smear another's character
and then wrap himself tightly in his Congressional immu-
nity."

Although the Dies Committee was supposed to be im-
partial, it immediately became a powerful propaganda
weapon for those who wanted to damn the New Deal as
a pawn of the Communists. Again and again it was charged
that "Communist" plays had been produced on the Federal
Theatre Project and that "Communistic" statements were
present in the writers project's state guides.

These attacks demoralized project workers—especially
because the White House did nothing to counteract them.
At first, Hopkins and Roosevelt did not take Dies seriously.
WPA headquarters refused to let the project chiefs rebut
the specific charges, and not until the November elections
did FDR see fit to denounce Dies's tactics. In December,
Flanagan and Alsberg were allowed to testify. Flanagan
boldly fought Dies for hours. Then Alsberg took the stand.
His manner, unlike hers, was conciliatory. Both chiefs
came with briefs which refuted point-by-point the charges
made against their projects. The committee, however, refused to include the briefs in its official record.

The public heard the Dies view of the arts projects, and

little more. His success in winning headlines prompted Congressman Clifton Woodrum, chairman of the House Appropriations Committee, to conduct another set of hearings in the spring of 1939, in order, he said, "to get the government out of the theatre business." Using some of the same witnesses as Dies, he zeroed in on the projects in New York City. Now it became a familiar routine: sensational charges, big headlines, damaging publicity.

Were there Communists on the projects? No one denied that some were there. Congress itself forbade discrimination against certified relief clients on the basis of political affiliation. How many there were, only the Communist party itself could have known. Certainly there were more "sympathizers" than members. The real question was not how many there were, but what they did on the arts projects—that was the only legitimate subject of inquiry.

Why did people become Communists in the thirties? Jane De Hart Mathews, in her study of the Federal Theatre Project, gives this answer:

Alienated from the strident, tawdry commercialism of the 'twenties and distressed by the evictions, breadlines, hunger marches and Hoovervilles of the 'thirties, they sought commitment through a movement that promised to save mankind from poverty and war at a time when millions were on relief and the Third Reich threatened the peace of the Western world. Not necessarily simple-minded or maladjusted, they regarded their commitment, to use Arthur Koestler's words, as the "logical extension of the progressive humanistic trend."

The most creative people among them, she said, "made a substantial contribution to the Federal Theatre without permitting political attachments to interfere with artistic efforts. Others, also capable, were less willing and able to maintain this separation." In any event, the Communists "were never able to gain control of the management of the Federal Theatre" she concluded. In large part, she says, the charges were false. Nevertheless, the Dies and Woodrum committees succeeded in killing a nationwide theater employing 9,000 needy workers.

After the Woodrum hearings, the House reported out a relief bill for 1939–40 "aimed at radicals," as *The New York Times* put it. Funds for the WPA were reduced, all relief personnel on the projects for eighteen months or more had to be dismissed, and a loyalty oath was required of new workers. The art, music, and writers projects were to continue only if they could secure local sponsorship. And the theater project was to be ended at once.

Supporters for Federal One rallied nationally to its defense. Every step that could be imagined to save the Federal Theatre Project was taken. But it was hopeless. The country was looking elsewhere. Now war seemed closer than ever. Austria and Czechoslovakia had succumbed to Hitler, and Poland seemed to be next. The national economy was improving as orders for war materials began flowing in. A world war would put millions of people to work and make relief unnecessary.

On June 30, the relief bill was adopted by Congress. The legislators who wanted to abolish the Federal Theatre had threatened to cut off funds for all 2.5 million WPA workers if the 8,000 theater workers were kept on. Roosevelt signed the bill. The Federal Theatre was ordered shut down immediately. Word reached the Adelphi Theatre in New York where the project musical *Sing for Your Supper* was being performed. After the hit song, "Papa's Got a Job," the performance was suddenly interrupted. Someone stepped to the footlights and said, "Yes, Papa had a job—but they're taking it away from him at twelve o'clock tonight!" As the last performance ended, audience and cast together sang "Auld Lang Syne."

The arts projects were now under the supervision of the states, which had to pay a fourth of the projects' costs. Creative production, the maintenance of skill, and rehabilitation, which had been stressed under federal control, gave way to service to local sponsors. To keep going, the artists had to please the sponsors. The unconventional, the daring, and the experimental were no longer encouraged and rarely tolerated.

By the middle of 1940, the arts projects were being hitched to the defense program. The artists, for instance, began building training aids, making posters for military bases, and decorating servicemen's clubs. The WPA community art centers held classes on camouflage for officers and gave crafts courses to enlisted men. The creative arts were soon supplanted by the practical arts. Many people on the projects began to find jobs in defense plants, or they joined the military. By mid-1943, all WPA projects were phased out.

15 FINALE
OR OVERTURE?

"Culture?" said one congressman in response to a plea for funds to continue the federal arts projects. "What the hell, let 'em have a pick and shovel!"

In 1939 that congressman voiced the feelings of many people. President Roosevelt himself—the sponsor of the most massive cultural aid program the United States had ever financed—admitted that indifference to the arts was widespread. "I suppose," he wrote, "these elected legislators are representing the view of their constituents, for the simple reason that the average voter does not yet appreciate the need of encouraging art, music, and literature. Unfortunately, there are too many people who think that this type of white collar worker ought to be put to work digging ditches like everybody else. . . ."

Thirty years and more have passed since the WPA projects were abolished. Today, public interest in culture is infinitely higher. In 1973, a nationwide survey of public attitudes toward the arts disclosed that nearly half of the American people would be willing to pay an additional $25 in taxes annually to maintain and operate cultural facilities such as theater, music, and art exhibitions. One out of three would pay an additional $50. And two out of three would pay a $5 cultural tax.

What would that amount to? The $5 tax, if paid by the willing two-thirds of the population, would amount to about $465 million a year. Americans are ready to subsidize the arts because nine out of ten, the survey found, believe it is important "to the quality of life in the community to have facilities such as museums, theatres and concert halls." (Half of them said that the arts were not readily available to them where they lived.)

There has been nothing like the WPA arts program for a long time. Money to sustain the arts continues to come from familiar sources: private patrons, foundations, corporations, and government—federal, state, and municipal. Yet the arts today are in "a neck-and-neck race with catastrophe," according to Eric Larrabee, then executive director of the New York State Council on the Arts. He said:

The arts in this country are, in fact, on a starvation diet. The institutions which nurture them are crushed between rising costs and rising demand for their services, and burdened as a result with income gaps which grow greater each year of continued inflation. Those that are lucky enough to have endowments are eating them away in the struggle to stay alive. Artists as professionals continue to be underpaid almost beyond belief, at levels which would horrify a self-respecting garbage collector.

Our major symphony orchestras have run deeper and deeper into debt, art museums have been closing or cutting their days and their hours for public access, dance companies have shortened their seasons, theater groups have canceled productions and performances; even public library services and programs are being curtailed.

All this at a time when audiences are growing. The trouble is, there isn't the money to meet the rising demand. When it comes to getting the funds they need, the arts come after science and education. If the consumer were asked to shoulder the burden of rising costs, it would require hiking ticket prices so high only the wealthy could afford to pay.

Funding for the performing arts threatens to become worse. Studying the financial trend of the arts, the Ford Foundation concluded that deficits are expected to increase threefold in the next seven years—and twice that amount if inflation continues.

The Ford Foundation itself has been by far the biggest benefactor of the arts. Since 1957, it has given some $260 million to the arts. Running a distant second and third in the same period have been the Rockefeller Foundation with $68 million and the Mellon Foundation with $43 million. That aid, together with the much smaller sums that hundreds of other foundations give, is indispensable. But it is still only a fraction of what is needed. The foundations are expected to give not more than 10 percent of the nation's total arts requirements in the near future.

The business community has offered help, making contributions to local art museums, theater companies, and symphonies. Much of this is only a token—a public-relations gesture. The giant corporations (such as Mobil, IBM, Exxon, Xerox, Philip Morris) have done more, underwriting costly television programs that feature the performing arts. Yet this is really a form of institutional advertising, and doesn't do much for the arts organizations beyond offering public exposure and a modest fee. If they wished to, they could do vastly more. Corporations may deduct up to 5 percent of their net income for philanthropy, but few go over 1 percent, and probably not more than a nickel out of every philanthropic dollar is given to the arts.

The states have recently begun to pay attention to the problem of sustaining the arts. New York State, far in advance of the others, doubled its allotment for the 1974–75 fiscal year, jumping from some $16 million a year to $34 million. But for 1976–77 it was cut back to $27.3 million. The goal now is to spread culture throughout the state while at the same time supplying more state funds to aid major cultural institutions. The Council on the Arts is required to provide at least 75 cents' worth of art services for each resident of each of the state's sixty-two counties. And with no compromise in quality. The effect in many cases is to fund the performances of a touring theater company or a symphony in counties where there is a dearth of professional groups.

What is especially encouraging about New York's program is that it sustains not only cultural organizations but the creative artist directly. The council, for example, commissions new works of music, with a performing organization choosing its own composer, putting up half the money, and guaranteeing beforehand to perform the finished work. It also offers grants to individual artists for choreography, theater, photography, literature, and filmmaking, asking in return that the grantee perform a community service in the artist's own field.

The handful of other states which budget significantly for culture have thus far appropriated only a million a year or less. Better than nothing, but only by a little. At least they have recognized a human need. One advocate of such aid wrote a letter to *The New York Times*, asking why support of the arts in America shouldn't be made "on the same basis that other everyday services are financed: education, health, police and fire service and sanitation. . . . The arts are now a necessity and should be made as extensively available as other basic public services. If Federal, state, and local governments follow this guideline, the arts will, indeed, become a part of the daily life of all the people."

What about the national government? Federal funds for the arts have been expanding ever since 1965, when the National Endowment for the Arts was established by Congress. And "contrary to the fears of those who thought [it] would be philistine in its posture and political in its control," said Robert Brustein, dean of the Yale School of Drama, "this agency now constitutes the most enlightened, as well as the most generous, source of support in the country."

Federal funds for the arts grew from $2.5 million in fiscal 1965 to $72 million in fiscal 1975. It sounds impressive, until you make comparisons. In a country of 230 million people, that $72 million comes to about 32 cents per person. Canada contributed $1.40 for each of its people that year, and West Germany, $2.40. For the theater alone, West Germany was spending $35 million a year! The United States contributes less to the arts per capita than any other major country.

The rapid climb in appropriations for the arts seemed to be slowing down by the mid-seventies. There is still suspicion of artists in Congress, and as inflation has soared, the legislators have begun resisting requests for bigger budgets.

Another problem to consider is the allocation of available funds. One wing pressures the National Endowment to distribute grants on the widest geographical basis, another insists that it support only quality performing groups. For example, should small sums be given to all 1,200 symphony orchestras in this country, or full support to the 12 greatest ones?

The National Endowment tries to do both, so that, as Brustein put it, "it manages to feed virtually everybody without filling anyone's belly." A symbol of the popular appeal it strives for is the "Artrain," which brought classic paintings to the countryside where no galleries exist. Aboard were living artists, too—sculptors, potters, silversmiths, macramémakers—who demonstrated their crafts to over 70 million children and adults in just one year. In dance, at one point, there were fifty companies touring forty states with Endowment support. The charter of the Arts Endowment calls for attention to both the fine arts and the folk arts.

Unlike the WPA arts projects, the Endowment does not put artists on a federal payroll. Grant policy is set by a national council of private citizens, most of them distinguished in the arts. Applications for aid are screened first by the staff, and then by panels of citizens representing the various arts. Finally, the survivors face the council's decision. None of the proposed projects can be profit-making, and the recipients must be both talented and in need of money to do the work. The question of talent and need are of course subject to interpretation. Grants run from a few hundred dollars for an individual to hundreds of thousands for an institution or organization. More than 2,000 grants were made in a single year recently.

But unfortunately, the solitary writer, composer, or painter gets much less attention than the performing artist when it comes to funding. A study of 350 creative artists who had won professional recognition (all of them had worked at the MacDowell Colony for artists at one time or another) showed that about half had earned less than $1,000 from what they had created in 1968. Of the painters and sculptors, only one in ten could support himself and his family on what the sales of his work brought in. The writers were somewhat better off: One in four could live on their earnings. The artists were not starving, they said. Most of them lived on the by-products of what they created (lecturing, performing, teaching, conducting, editing). So they managed, but most of them poorly.

The new patronage of the seventies—public and private —has altered this picture somewhat. But not nearly enough. I think most artists do not want the state to take over the arts. Looking about the world, they have seen what total control has done to cripple or destroy art and artists. Their attitude is probably like the response given by the MacDowell artists, as reported by Russell Lynes:

> Through all the answers run an absolute confidence that what the art-makers do is essential to their own salvation and equally essential to the salvation of the society in which they somehow manage to live. They do not ask to be pampered; they do not want to be social parasites; they desperately want to be allowed the time to work and to be respected and remunerated for what they have to do.

In the days of the WPA the artists were not pampered. Nor were they made into social parasites. Just as the nation tapped the vast natural resources of the Tennessee River Valley, so did it reclaim the powerful creative energies of its hungry artists. Both experiments taught us much in the development of public policy and program. We learned that support of the arts, like reclamation of the land, is not only a legitimate but a desirable function of government.

So many patterns for government aid to the arts have been shaped at home and abroad since the thirties that we need no longer look to the WPA arts projects as the sole model for the future. But the achievements recorded in their short lifetime are as important to the history of society as they are to the history of the arts. The WPA broke the vacuum in which American artists had worked, discovering immense audiences only dreamed of before. The arts, for the first time, entered the life of the community. It is a connection we need to nourish.

Bibliography

I owe the best parts of this book to those men and women who worked on the WPA arts projects and were willing to share their experiences. Some of them I was able to interview; others were kind enough to write to me. Still others have put their memoirs into print. I combed all the autobiographies I could find that contained references to life on the projects. It might have been as little as a few lines or as much as a detailed chapter. But it always helped, and I gratefully acknowledge it here.

A lot has been written about the Great Depression itself, but little about the four arts projects. One book (see McDonald below) covers all of them, but in an academic manner. It is useful chiefly to the scholar. There seems to be almost nothing about the music project.

In addition to the sources listed, I used the contemporary press and periodicals, including the specialized publications for each of the arts. I also referred to the *Congressional Record* and to the reports of House and Senate committee hearings on the WPA.

Finally, I have put into this book some of my own

recollections of the Depression years, and of my first adult job on the Federal Theatre Project. There I stayed for three years.

This bibliography includes many of the sources used in preparing this book and offers suggestions for further reading. An asterisk marks books available in paperback.

THE DEPRESSION

*Bird, Caroline. *The Invisible Scar*. New York: McKay, 1960.

*Congdon, Don (ed.). *The Thirties: A Time to Remember*. New York: Simon & Schuster, 1962.

*Filler, Louis (ed.). *The Anxious Years: America in the 1930s*. New York: Capricorn, 1964.

*Freidel, Frank. *The New Deal and the American People*. Englewood Cliffs, N.J.: Prentice-Hall, 1964.

*Leuchtenberg, William E. *Franklin D. Roosevelt and the New Deal*. New York: Harper & Row, 1963.

*Meltzer, Milton. *Brother, Can You Spare a Dime? The Great Depression, 1929–1933*. New York: Knopf, 1969.

*Shannon, David A. (ed.). *The Great Depression*. Englewood Cliffs, N.J.: Prentice-Hall, 1960.

*Terkel, Studs. *Hard Times: An Oral History of the Great Depression*. New York: Pantheon, 1970.

Wilson, Edmund. *The American Earthquake*. New York: Doubleday, 1958.

GENERAL

McDonald, William F. *Federal Relief Administration and the Arts*. Columbus, Ohio: Ohio State University Press, 1969.

THEATER

*Abramson, Doris E. *Negro Playwrights and the American Theatre, 1925–1959*. New York: Columbia University Press, 1969. (Chapter 3, on the thirties.)

Flanagan, Hallie. *Arena*. New York: Duell, Sloan and Pearce, 1940.

Goldstein, Malcolm. *The Political Stage: American Drama and Theatre of the Great Depression*. New York: Oxford University Press, 1974. (Chapter 9, on the Federal Theatre.)

Himelstein, Morgan Y. *Drama Was a Weapon: The Left-Wing Theatre in New York, 1929–1941*. New Brunswick, N.J.: Rutgers University Press, 1963.

Houseman, John. *Run-Through*. New York: Simon & Schuster, 1972.

Mathews, Jane De Hart. *The Federal Theatre: 1935–1939*. Princeton, N.J.: Princeton University Press, 1967.

Mitchell, Loften. *Black Drama: The Story of the Negro in the Theatre*. New York: Hawthorn, 1967.

Rabkin, Gerald. *Drama and Commitment: Politics in the American Theatre of the Thirties*. Bloomington, Ind.: Indiana University Press, 1964.

Rice, Elmer. *The Living Theatre*. New York: Harper & Row, 1959. (Chapter 13 on the Federal Theatre.)

deRohan, Pierre (ed.). *Federal Theatre Plays*. 2 vols. New York: Random House, 1938.

ART

McKinzie, Richard D. *The New Deal for Artists*. Princeton, N.J.: Princeton University Press, 1973.

*O'Connor, Francis V. (ed.). *Art for the Millions: Essays from the 1930s by Artists and Administrators of the WPA Federal Art Project.* Boston: New York Graphic Art Society, 1973.
O'Connor, Francis V. (ed.). *The New Deal Art Projects: An Anthology of Memoirs.* Washington, D.C.: Smithsonian Institution, 1972.

MUSIC

Engel, Lehman. *This Bright Day.* New York: Macmillan, 1973.

WRITING

*Mangione, Jerre. *The Dream and the Deal: The Federal Writers Project. 1935–1943.* Boston: Little, Brown, 1972.
*Salzman, Jack (ed.). *Years of Protest: A Collection of American Writing of the 1930's.* New York: Pegasus, 1967.
*Swados, Harvey (ed.). *The American Writer and the Great Depression.* Indianapolis, Ind.: Bobbs Merrill, 1966.

For a list of the "American Guide Series" and other volumes produced by the Federal Writers Project, see Mangione, pp. 375–96.

INDEX

Abbott, Berenice, 79
Agee, James, 130
Aiken, Conrad, 116
Algren, Nelson, 116–117, 122
Alsberg, Henry, 20, 21, 104–
106, 107, 110, 115, 118,
124, 127, 128, 132, 138
Alston, Charles, 87
American Guide Series, 103–
104, 105, 106, 107, 108–
115
Appel, Benjamin, 102
Arent, Arthur, 34, 36, 37
Art education, 84–89
Artists: *see* federal projects;
economic problems of,
53–56, 148; on relief, 55–56;
subsidies to, 142–149; and
WPA, 53–90
Artists Union, 66, 67, 133
Arts, funding for, *see* cultural
aid programs, federal
projects
Attaway, William, 121
Authors, *see* Writers

Authors Guild, 20
Authors League of America,
103

Baker, Jacob, 20
Barber, Philip, 28
Bay, Howard, 37
Bearden, Romare, 87, 88
Bellow, Saul, 116
Bennett, Gwendolyn, 87
Benton, Thomas Hart, 55, 65
Biddle, George, 20
Black studies, 123–127
Blacks, 12, 28; on art project,
46–48; dismissals of, 124;
numbers employed by
WPA, 120; and slavery
studies, 124–127; struggle
against discrimination, 124–
125; on theatre project, 46–
48; on writers project, 112,
121–127
Blankfort, Michael, 29
Blitzstein, Marc, 40, 42, 95

Bontemps, Arna, 123
Botkin, Benjamin, 116, 126–127, 130
Brown, Milton W., 86
Brown, Sterling, 47, 112, 116, 121, 123–124
Browne, Rosalind Bengelsdorf, 67
Brustein, Robert, 146, 147
Business: subsidy to arts, 144–145

Cahill, Holger, 20, 21, 56–57, 59, 62, 69, 80, 81, 83
Caldwell, Erskine, 130
Cayton, Horace, 121
Censorship, 38–44, 52, 109–111, 126
Cheever, John, 116
Children, art classes for, 86; music classes for, 97–98; theater for, 45, 46, 48–49
Christensen, Erwin O., 84
Clarke, Harold H., 29
College Art Association, 55, 56
Communism, 5, 110, 137–140
Community art centers, 84–89, 141
Composers, 95–97
Composers Forum Laboratory, 96
Conkle, E. P., 39
Conrad, Earl, 133
Conroy, Jack, 116
Corey, Paul, 116
Corporations, aid to arts, 144–145
Couch, W. T., 107, 130
Cowley, Malcolm, 101, 102

Cradle Will Rock, The, 40–43, 48, 95
Crichlow, Ernest, 87
Cronbach, Robert, 26, 73–75
Cronyn, George, 106
Crosby, Alexander, 102–103, 109–110, 112–113, 115
Cultural aid programs, 142–149

Dahlberg, Edward, 116
da Silva, Howard, 40
Davis, Stuart, 65, 70, 78
Dehn, Adolph, 78
de Kooning, Willem, 70–71
Depression, 1–15
de Rivera, José, 75
Dies, Martin, 137–140
Dramatists, 27–29, 34, 38, 47, 48, 50
DuBois, W. E. B., 125
Dwight, Mabel, 60

Eiseley, Loren, 116
Elections: of 1932, 10; of 1934, 12; of 1936, 134; of 1938, 138
Ellison, Ralph, 116, 122, 123
Engel, Lehman, 94–95
Evans, Walker, 130
Evergood, Philip, 63

Fascism, 51–52, 137
Fearing, Kenneth, 116
Feder, Abe, 37
Federal Art Project (WPA), 19, 56–90, 115; and abstractionists, 64, 67–68, 78; allocation of works, 61; and art education, 84–89; attacks upon, 72–73; blacks

on, 86–88; and community art centers, 84–89; and easel painters, 62–68; and expressionists, 64–65, 78; and folk art, 80–84; and graphic arts, 76–80; and Index of American Design, 81–84; influence of, 61; innovations by, 66, 78–79; and muralists, 54, 65, 68–73; numbers employed by, 58, 77, 82; and photography, 79; production required by, 59–60, 77, 88; protests dismissals from, 135; qualifications for, 58–59; reaches children, 86; record of, 62, 79, 82, 85, 87; and regionalists, 64; and sculptors, 73–75; and social themes, 63, 72; wage rates, 59, 88

Federal Music Project (WPA), 19, 91–99; builds symphony orchestras, 93–94; and composers, 95–97; collects folk music, 99; concert branch of, 93; dismissals from, 136; and music copying, 91; and music education, 93; numbers employed by, 93; offers music classes, 97–98; qualifications for, 93; record of, 91, 93, 95, 97; retrains music teachers, 97–98; ticket prices, 95; wage rate, 95

Federal Project Number One, 19, 20, 57, 92, 104, 106, 135, 136, 140

Federal Theatre Project (WPA), 15, 16–17, 23–52,

95; appeals to children, 45, 46, 48–49; aid to therapy, 49; blacks in, 29, 46–48; and classics, 50; dismissals from, 132, 134; and historical drama, 49–50; and Living Newspaper, 30–39; numbers employed by, 45, 140; and playwrights unit, 27–28; and social issues, 25, 27, 28–29, 30–39; ticket prices, 30, 48; and vaudeville, 45–46, 48; wages paid by, 17

Federal Writers Project (WPA), 19, 100–131; blacks on, 121–127; and censorship, 109–111; congressional investigations of, 118; dismissals from, 118, 124, 133, 134; influence on documentary, 130–131; Living Lore unit, 128–130; numbers employed, 105; press hostile to, 110, 118; produces guidebooks, 108–115, 123; production required, 117; qualifications for, 104, state directors of, 106; studies of slavery, 124–127; uses oral history, 125, 130–131; wage rates, 106, 117, 122

Ferber, Herbert, 75
Fisher, Rudolph, 48
Fisher, Vardis, 111
Fisk University, 125, 127
Flanagan, Hallie, 17, 20, 21, 24, 25, 27, 30, 32, 33, 36, 39, 40, 41, 43, 44, 45, 51, 52, 138

Folk arts, 57, 80–84, 99, 123
Folklore, 127–130
Ford Foundation, 144
Foundations: aid to arts, 144
Frank, Yasha, 48

Gaer, Joseph, 106
Gassner, John, 33
Geer, Will, 40
Gibson, William, 116, 117–118
Glassgold, C. Adolph, 82
Gold, Michael, 29
Gorky, Arshile, 70
Graphic arts, 76–80
Green, Paul, 49
Guggenheim Fellowships, 112, 123
Gwathmey, Robert, 63

Hall-Rogers, Thomas, 29
Halpert, Herbert, 99
Hare, David, 75
Harlem Art Center, 87
Harlem Art Workshop, 88
Harlem Artists Guild, 86
Harnett, William, 83
Harris, Reed, 106
Hastings, Milo, 29
Hayden, Robert, 121
Hebald, Milton, 75
Hess, Thomas B., 89
Hetter, Dora Thea, 118
Hirsch, Joseph, 63
Hitler, Adolf, 10, 29, 40, 51, 137, 140
Hoover, Herbert, 3, 4, 5, 9, 10, 11
Hopkins, Harry, 13, 18, 20, 21, 24, 25, 36–37, 39, 60, 105, 110, 134, 138
Horn, Axel, 54, 65, 66

Hornung, Clarence P., 84
House Committee on Un-American Activities, 137–140
Houseman, John, 25, 27, 29, 40–43, 47, 48
Hughes, Langston, 123
Hurston, Zora Neale, 121, 123

Income, in 1920s, 2; 1930s, 3
Index of American Composers, 96
Index of American Design, 81–84
Irvine, Harry, 30
It Can't Happen Here, 51–52

Javitz, Romana, 81
Johnson, Fenton, 122
Johnson, John H., 122

Kainen, Jacob, 54, 57–58, 78, 80
Kapuscinski, Richard, 91
Kazin, Alfred, 114
Kees, Weldon, 116
Kellock, Katherine, 106
Knaths, Karl, 70
Knotts, Benjamin, 82
Koch, Howard, 27–28
Kuniyoshi, Yasuo, 78

LaGuardia, Fiorello, 135
Laning, Edward, 70
Lantz, Louis, 49
Larrabee, Eric, 143
Lashin, Orrie, 29
Lawrence, Jacob, 63, 87–89

Levin, Jack, 63
Levitt, Saul, 116
Lewis, Norman, 87
Lewis, Sinclair, 51
Library of Congress, 96, 99, 126–127
Lipschitz, Jacques, 75
Lipton, Seymour, 75
Living Newspaper, 30–39
Lomax, John A., 125–126, 127
Long, Huey, 51, 137
Losey, Joseph, 36
Loyalty oath, 140
Lynes, Russell, 148

MacDowell Colony, 147–148
MacLeod, Norman, 116
Madrigal Singers, 94–95
Mangione, Jerre, 104, 105, 116, 118
Marin, John, 65
Mason, Daniel Gregory, 94
Mathews, Jane DeHart, 139–140
McClendon, Rose, 47
McDonald, William F., 44
McHugh, Vincent, 116
McKay, Claude, 121, 123
McKinzie, Richard D., 64, 136
McMahon, Audrey, 56, 60, 77, 135
Mellon Foundation, 144
Mercury Theatre, 28
Morrell, Peter, 48
Morris, Lawrence, 106
Moss, Carlton, 48
Motley, Willard, 116
Muralists, 54, 60, 61, 65, 68–73
Museum of Modern Art, 57, 71, 79

Musicians, 19, 20; on relief, 92; unemployment of, 92; on music project, 91–99
Mussolini, Benito, 29, 39, 51, 137

National Endowment for the Arts, 146–147
National Gallery of Art, 84
Neel, Alice, 64
New Deal, 11, 12, 110, 133, 138
New York State Council on the Arts, 143, 145
New York Times, The, 30, 36, 38, 111, 131, 140, 145
Newspaper Guild, 20, 32
Nurnberg, Maxwell, 29

O'Connor, Francis V., 54
O'Neill, Eugene, 50–51
Oral history, 125, 130–131
Oroczo, José Clemente, 65
Ottley, Roi, 121

Painters, 20, 55, 60, 61, 62–68
Partnow, Hyde, 129
Pettis Ashley, 96
Phillips, Ulrich B., 125
Pollock, Jackson, 55–56, 63–64, 65, 66
Pratt Institute, 54
Prestopino, Gregorio, 63
Public Works of Art Project, 20

Quirt, Walter, 63

"Red menace", 137–140
Reddick, Lawrence D., 124–125

Reeves, Ruth, 81, 82
Reisman, Philip, 63
Relief, 3, 4, 6, 12, 13, 14, 16, 17, 18, 21, 55–56; conflict with art, 21–22, 26, 57; conflict with politics, 21–22, 57, 59; qualifying for, 58–59
Rexroth, Kenneth, 116
Rice, Elmer, 28, 39, 43
Rivera, Diego, 65
Rockefeller Foundation, 144
Roosevelt, Eleanor, 25
Roosevelt, Franklin D., 10, 11, 13, 18, 39, 56, 72, 110, 134, 135, 137, 138, 142
Rorty, James, 130
Rose, Barbara, 61
Rose, Herman, 64, 70
Rosenberg, Harold, 89, 116
Rosenfeld, Isaac, 116
Roskolenko, Harry, 116
Roszak, Theodore, 75
Rothko, Mark, 64
Rourke, Constance, 67, 82, 84

St. Joseph, Ellis, 28
Saul, Oscar, 49
Savage, Augusta, 87, 88
Schanker, Louis, 70, 79
Sculptors, 20, 26, 60, 73–75
Shahn, Ben, 65
Siqueiros, David Alfaro, 65, 66
Sklar, George, 29
Slave narratives, 124
Slavery, WPA studies of, 124–127
Sloan, John, 53
Smith, David, 75, 89
Smith, J. A., 48
Smith, Joseph Lindon, 83

Smithsonian Institution, 84
Smithsonian Museum, 54
Sokoloff, Nikolai, 20, 21, 92–93
Solman, Joseph, 55, 63, 64
Somervell, Brehon, 135
Soyer, David, 72
Soyer, Moses, 71–72
Soyer, Raphael, 71, 78
States: subsidy to arts, 145
Stavis, Barrie, 29
Stavis, Leona, 29
Stock market crash, 1
Suicides, 6, 7, 133, 136
Sundgaard, Arnold, 38

Terkel, Studs, 116, 131
Theater, *see* Federal Theatre Project; on Broadway, 24–25; for children, 26; community, 24; experimental, 25; regional, 24–25; and social issues, 25, 27; unemployment in, 7, 23–24; university, 24; and WPA, 24–52
Theatre for Youth, 48
Thomas, J. Parnell, 39
Thrash, Dox, 78
Twain, Mark, 49
Tworkov, Jack, 64

Unemployed Writers Association, 20
Unemployment, 2, 3, 4, 12, 13

Vaudeville, 23, 45–46, 48
Velonis, Anthony, 78
Veterans bonus, 9–10

Walker, Margaret, 116, 121
Ward, Lem, 38
Watson, Morris, 32
Weber, Max, 65
Welles, Orson, 29, 40–43
Whitney, Gertrude
    Vanderbilt, 56
Whitney Museum, 56
Williams, Aubrey, 19
Willison, George, 116
Wilson, Edmund, 130
Wilson, Frank, 48
Woodrum, Clifton, 139, 140
Woodson, Carter G., 125
Woodward, C. Vann, 126
Workers Alliance, 132
Works Progress Administra-
    tion (WPA), and art, 53–
    90; and the arts, 19–22;
    costs of, 17, 19; director of,
    13; dismissals by, 132–141;
    and music, 91–99; members
    employed by, 140; origin of,
13; phased out, 141; pro-
    grams of, 13; rationale for,
    18–19; requires loyalty oath,
    140; and theater, 23–52;
    wages paid by, 17; and
    writers, 100–131
WPA, *see* Works Progress Ad-
    ministration
WPA Joint Committee on
    Folk Arts, 130
Wright, Richard, 116, 122–123
Writers, 20, 26; economic
    problems of, 100–102, 148;
    jobless, 103; on federal writ-
    ers project, 100–131
Writers Union, 20, 133

Yerby, Frank, 122

Zadkine, Ossip, 75